Boston Unitarianism

Also from Westphalia Press
westphaliapress.org

The Idea of the Digital University

Bulwarks Against Poverty in America

Treasures of London

Avate Garde Politician

L'Enfant and the Freemasons

Baronial Bedrooms

Making Trouble for Muslims

Philippine Masonic Directory ~ 1918

Paddle Your Own Canoe

Opportunity and Horatio Alger

Careers in the Face of Challenge

Bookplates of the Kings

Hymns to the Gods

Freemasonry in Old Buffalo

Original Cables from the Pearl Harbor Attack

Social Satire and the Modern Novel

The Essence of Harvard

The Genius of Freemasonry

A Definitive Commentary on Bookplates

James Martineau and Rebuilding Theology

Bohemian San Francisco

The Wizard

Crime 3.0

Anti-Masonry and the Murder of Morgan

Understanding Art

Spies I Knew

Lodge "Himalayan Brotherhood" No. 459 C.E.

Ancient Masonic Mysteries

Collecting Old Books

Masonic Secret Signs and Passwords

Death Valley in '49

Lariats and Lassos

Mr. Garfield of Ohio

The Wisdom of Thomas Starr King

The French Foreign Legion

War in Syria

Naturism Comes to the United States

New Sources on Women and Freemasonry

Designing, Adapting, Strategizing in Online Education

Gunboat and Gun-runner

Memoirs of a Poor Relation

Espionage!

Bohemian San Francisco

Tales of Old Japan

Boston Unitarianism
1820-1850

A Study of the Life and Work of
Nathaniel Langdon Frothingham

by Octavius Brooks Frothingham

WESTPHALIA PRESS
An imprint of Policy Studies Organization

Boston Unitarianism, 1820-1850: A Study of the Life and Work of Nathaniel Langdon Frothingham
All Rights Reserved © 2014 by Policy Studies Organization

Westphalia Press
An imprint of Policy Studies Organization
1527 New Hampshire Ave., NW
Washington, D.C. 20036
info@ipsonet.org

ISBN-13: 978-1-63391-088-1
ISBN-10: 1633910881

Cover design by Taillefer Long at Illuminated Stories:
www.illuminatedstories.com

Daniel Gutierrez-Sandoval, Executive Director
PSO and Westphalia Press

Rahima Schwenkbeck, Director of Marketing and Media
PSO and Westphalia Press

Updated material and comments on this edition
can be found at the Westphalia Press website:
www.westphaliapress.org

BOSTON UNITARIANISM

1820–1850

A STUDY OF THE LIFE AND WORK

OF

NATHANIEL LANGDON FROTHINGHAM

BY

OCTAVIUS BROOKS FROTHINGHAM

A Sketch

NEW YORK & LONDON
G. P. PUTNAM'S SONS
The Knickerbocker Press
1890

CONTENTS.

	PAGE
PREFATORY NOTE	
I.—THREE TYPES OF UNITARIANISM	1
II.—AN EXAMPLE	15
III.—THE FIRST CHURCH	26
IV.—THE DOGMATICAL POSITION	37
V.—LITERATURE AND RELIGION	70
VI.—THE UNITARIAN LAYMAN	93
VII.—THE OLD WORLD	129
VIII.—THE FREEDOM OF FRIENDSHIP	159
IX.—THE BOSTON ASSOCIATION OF CONGREGATIONAL MINISTERS	213
X.—THE END	228

PREFATORY NOTE.

A WORD of explanation seems to be necessary. Many years ago I proposed writing something in memory of Dr. Frothingham, but abandoned the project on account of the meagreness of the biographical material. Within the twelvemonth, a warm friend and admirer of his asked me to prepare a memoir. Then the matter was reviewed once more, and it occurred to me that some reminiscences of my father might be woven into a sketch of his time. This has been attempted, with what success others must judge. So much is certain, that if I did not undertake the task nobody else would. This will account for the mixture of denominational concerns with personal details. It is needless to say that the author writes as an historian, not as an advocate.

O. B. F.

BOSTON UNITARIANISM.

I.

THREE TYPES OF UNITARIANISM.

IT has long seemed to me that justice was not done to the Unitarianism which lay between William Ellery Channing on one side, and Theodore Parker on the other; the simple *rationalism* as distinguished from the *spiritualism* of the former, and the *naturalism* of the latter; literary Unitarianism it might be called; the religion of sentiment, feeling, emotion; the religion of unadorned good-sense. The fame of these two men so far eclipsed the others, that they sank into general obscurity, and were almost unknown outside of a small circle of admirers, while their influence, if acknowledged at all, was considered insignificant. By many they were regarded as drones, respectable good-for-nothings. Yet, it is my belief, the freedom and ease of movement in the mind of this generation, its elasticity, its gracefulness, its love of musical expression, its demand for finish in thought and phrase, its modest demeanor in presence of deep problems, must be in great measure due to them. Of course, some were more distinguished than others, but chiefly in distinct fields—as James Walker in philosophy, John G. Palfrey in history, Alexander Young in biography,—but as a class of thinkers they held no eminent place. It is the fashion to depreciate them, to deny them power, to esteem them of small account. That they were destitute of positive, new, creative force, is freely admitted; but that they were without formative genius or power, is not so easily granted. It was their office to create an atmosphere rather than to advance a cause, to diffuse a spirit of liberality rather than to promote the interests of a system of thought, whether doctrinal or philosophical. They were not organizers; they were not sectaries; they were not champions of any school; they were not possessed by any dominant idea; they had no passion for social reform. They were simply scholars and gentlemen; dignified, gracious, genuine, sweet; fond of elegant studies, of good English, of courteous ways, of poetic expression, of the amenities of life. They were conservative of existing institutions in so far as they allowed the free movement of cultivated mind, and desired no change except in the direction of mental emancipation. They pushed against no barriers that did not limit the right to walk over all the fields of literature, unimpeded and unchallenged. For the rest, they were contented with things as they were and disliked innovation, dreading the intrusion of untried ideas; agitation, violence, vehemence, even in the advocacy of just principles, they deplored. They believed in the prevalence of sweetness and light. Such men are never creators or leaders.

That William E. Channing was the father of spiritual Christianity admits of no question. The fact is undisputed. His immense and growing fame, the dedication of churches in his honor, the association of his name with the sect, the acclaim of its most eminent men, preachers, critics, thinkers, the steady increase of his noblest teachings, while his limitations have been gradually falling away, the development of his cardinal thoughts—upward, inward, outward—all attest this. Admitting the substantial justice of M. Renan's criticism; granting that Channing did not think himself clear on several doctrinal matters; conceding that he was but half developed as a philosopher; it is nevertheless true that he was the inspirer of the most exalted souls in the denomination. And this may be easily explained. The insignificance of his physical frame, its weakness and infirmity, made him seem a spirit, the more so on account of his untiring pursuit of knowledge and his habitual absorption in high themes, which he clung to and persisted in long after strong people would have abandoned the quest in sheer fatigue. Dr. Dewey, in a discourse delivered after Channing's death, said: "On my first acquaintance with him, it was my happiness to pass a number of weeks under his own roof. His health was then delicate; he went abroad but little; his mind was left untouched by the frailty of his body; and I found it constantly occupied and struggling with great questions, as the highest philosophy, or the highest religion, or the highest freedom of life; all the day long he pursued the questions which those themes present, without ever slackening or ever turning aside to ordinary and commonplace talk. The range of his subjects was as great as their character: from the most recondite point in philosophy—the difference between relative and absolute truth—to the forms of philanthropic enterprise and political thought around him. But his favorite themes were MAN and the NEW TESTAMENT; man, his condition, and the philosophy of his condition; the New Testament, Jesus Christ, his teaching, and the sublimest contemplation of God. Sometimes his mind was upon the same theme, almost without interruption, for an entire week; yet there was never any weariness in listening, but the weariness of exhaustion." He had his limitations, but his incessant endeavor to surmount them reduced them to a negative, subordinate, ephemeral position, like the clouds that obscure the rising sun and must soon be burned away, however solid they look. He was not a man of mere opinions— notions that lay on the surface of his mind and were driven about by the varying winds of doctrine, owing their temporary place, to the book he last read, or the person he last conversed with, but he was a man of deep convictions, which were rooted in his character, had an organic growth, and threw off dogmas as the chambered nautilus throws off its covering,

"Leaving its outgrown shell by life's unresting sea."

Such a man is of slow increase. His maturity is in the future. He is a seed rather than a forest. Channing said well, when, in answer to one who asked toward the end of his life what he considered to be the happiest period of his existence, he replied with a smile, "About the age of sixty." His true life did begin after his death.

At the bottom of his heart was a passion for pure religion, undefiled by rite or doctrine. It was the only passion he had, a real thirst for the Living God. The paternal nature of God was his cardinal belief, and it was his sole endeavor to explain this and render it vital in all its implications. This principle furnished a basis for his doctrine of an inherent dignity in man; of the divine Sonship of Jesus Christ, and his mission as the inspirer, friend, exemplar of the soul; of the Bible as conveying the Father's benignant will; of the immortal destiny as a demand of the spiritual part which presupposed a deathless continuance; of all reasonable attempts to elevate society. This alone justified the hope of temporal and eternal good. In fact, his central conviction was the love of God. The invincible optimism it aroused never left him. He had a genuine enthusiasm for truth, mental freedom and moral excellence. He was "always young for liberty." Miss Peabody reports him as saying: "I would not for the world interrupt or check your thought. . . . I would not for the world throw a damper on earnestness of inquiry; it is only by grappling with great questions that there can be any progress." His intimate friends say that he possessed a fine imagination, that he had a nice sense of color and lines. But this faculty was never unfolded. He was never a poet, except as every idealist must be one at heart. The tendency of his mind was toward philosophical speculation, and the bent of his will was in the direction of practical evils to be removed. His songs were spiritual. He thought more of the goodness in nature than of its beauty. That Washington Allston, his brother-in-law, prized his opinion of pictures, simply proves the existence of artistic sensibility in the constitution. The aim was spiritual, all the time, and attests the spirituality of Allston's art, quite as much as Channing's taste in praising. The man cared nothing about Unitarianism, simply because he abhorred division, and professed it merely on account of its unpopularity. His whole concern was with religion, not even with Christianity otherwise than as it was, in his estimation, the highest form of religion, the most potent instrument for cultivating the human soul. Of intellectual accomplishments, of literary finish, of philosophical talent, of learning, of scholarship, of criticism, he had no opinion whatever, unless as aids to a divine purpose.

Technically, Dr. Channing belonged to the Scotch system of philosophy—that of common-sense—dry, prosaic, unimaginative. But, really, he was a disciple of the intuitive school; nor is it at all surprising that the transcendentalism of a later epoch was derived from that adoring soul; that George Ripley borrowed an impulse from him; that Mr. Emerson, even, was indebted to him for inspiration. The intuitive philosophy would appear to be most consistent with Channing's leading ideas—with his interior or subjective conception of God as a Father, with his moral view of Christ as the perfect man, with his doctrine of a similarity of nature between the human and the divine spirit, with his interpretation of the Bible as a message of love to the mind of man—his reading of the heart's natural compassion into the text being well known. It was his main objection to the doctrine of hell that it outraged every instinctive feeling of justice and mercy. On one occasion, when an objector cited the "woe unto you scribes and pharisees" as an evidence that Jesus was not always animated by absolute kindness, he took down the New Testament and, rendering the Greek into "alas for you," gave a new meaning to the passage. Miss Peabody mentions the case of a young man who flung in his teeth the declaration, "Ye are of your father the devil." Dr. Channing paraphrased the verse, and then repeated it in a tone that conveyed earnestness alone, without a trace of anger. "Oh," said the young man, "if Jesus spoke *in that way* I have no doubts." In this instance, as in a great many others, Dr. Channing assumed the superiority of the affections. Love being the highest principle, he took that for his chief authority against historical probability.

Channing, therefore, stood at one extreme, as the illustration of spiritual aspiration. At the other extreme stood Theodore Parker, an illustration of the power of practical will. With every disposition to grant Mr. Parker's extraordinary force and eminent service; with the heartiest admission of his claim upon admiration and love; with grateful acknowledgment of his integrity, singleness of mind, outspokenness, courage, unaffected warm-heartedness, tenderness of feeling, catholicity of sentiment—his talent was practical, not speculative. He was an enormous reader, but not a subtle thinker. He had a prodigious memory, but not a penetrating intellect or soaring imagination. Though he honored Dr. Channing, listened reverently to him, spoke beautifully of him in a funeral discourse, he probably never caught his genius, or fully comprehended his mind. Mr. Parker kept a record of every thing, had an outside acquaintance with all systems, could put his finger on every significant name or passage, but his ability to describe opinions was out of proportion to his inward appreciation of them. He was not complex. He was not seraphic. He was not aërial or winged. Terrestrial he essentially was; not, by any means, "of the earth, earthy," for no one was ever more clean, heroic, devoted, than he; no one was more consecrated to the most exalted human aims. But he must have *human* aims. He was practical, executive, charged with stern mental force, a Titan, not an angel, a Briareus with a hundred *hands*. One has only to read his "Discourse on Religion" to see how *muscular* his persuasions were. In the early days of the Transcendental discussion, it was evident that this "Orson of parsons" used the new philosophy as a club wherewith to belabor his opponents. To a friend he said, as Luther said to Melancthon, "I was born to thunder and lighten, and break things down to the ground." He was an agitator by temperament. It is often said, that the Unitarian controversy and the anti-slavery movement diverted him from his ultimate work. That they diverted him from his ulterior *design* is quite possible; but that they injured his actual *achievement* may be doubted. He misapprehended his own office, which was to destroy, not to build up. In reality these convulsions were his opportunity. They called forth his characteristic qualities, his directness, his frankness, his eloquence of speech, his wit, his sarcasm, his bluntness of sentiment, his invective, his power of denunciation and contempt. His closet-writing would never probably have been of great value, nor would he have been famous as a scholar. He thought of himself as a reformer of faith, a seond Luther. William E. Channing was "cautious and timid both in thought and action," in his view. There was no reform in which he did not take a part, and the air was thick with the breath of change. Every institution rushed to judgment. "In the history of the world," said Emerson then, "the doctrine of reform had never such hope as at the present hour." It was the abstract conscience against all conventionalities. The result of which was a complete overturning of all social arrangements; for these were placed at the mercy of individual caprice, the gathered usage of the past not being accepted as authority. It should be added that Mr. Parker was not always on the destructive side. He had conservative leanings, for personal feeling is apt to be conservative, and his personal feelings were very strong. For instance, he attended the anti-Sabbath convention, and made a speech in favor of the Sunday. Still he took part in it, as Dr. Channing did not, though the latter was present as a listener, and in so doing admitted the principle that the private soul may pronounce on institutions, a doctrine that offended the more deliberate judgment of a large number of his contemporaries. Parker was a headlong man. Fortunately his impulses were all noble, and his tremendous force of will was directed in humane paths, and was made a power of justice. At the time, however, this could not be generally seen, even by such as were in sympathy with the ultimate aim, as Channing certainly was; while the more timid or prudent, or thoughtful, or lukewarm, turned away in disgust, under an impression that the problems were too delicate for any summary treatment, and must be left to the slow working of reason.

To this last class belonged the Unitarians I would describe, a class of men who lay between Channing and Parker, lacking the fervent spirituality of the one, and the impassioned earnestness of the other; men of quiet culture and scholarship, of elegant tastes, refined manners, and dignified conduct; social, affable, amiable, kind, gentle, but not in the smallest degree volcanic, or sulphureous, or explosive with wrath, however "holy." This type of clergyman is admirably depicted in Dr. Frothingham's tribute to his friend, Dr. Lunt, prepared for the Massachusetts Historical Society. He used these words: "In theology, Dr. Lunt stood far on the right wing, though not on the extreme right, of the Unitarian denomination. Reverence for antiquity and established belief, for the early Church and the sacred associations of the past, wrought strongly within him. He loved to hold fast, so far as he could, to the language of Scripture, and to the doctrine, liberally interpreted, which had come down from the fathers. He was more ready to accept than anxious to define hallowed phrases. While he was open to new light, he was jealous of innovations. He shrank from all approach to the subversive speculations of the newest criticism. While he repelled with every power of his intellect, every instinct of his conscience, every throb of his heart, the dogmas of Calvinistic divinity, yet his Puritan soul leaned back, as far as it dared, toward ancient formulas. . . . The political and reformatory movements of the day he was slow to admit into his pulpit. Controversial religion was not to his liking. The Biblical neologies of our new times were an offense, if not an alarm to him. He held the literal word reverently dear, although he endeavored to give it an expansive scope, and sought underneath it the most spiritual significances." Nothing could be more exact than this so far as it goes. But it should be added, that the faith we are concerned with laid stress on the old virtues of private character—purity, moderation, kindness, hospitality, generosity, peacefulness, hopefulness, humility, truth —rather than on the philosophical foundations of belief, or the changes necessary to perfect society. Its whole purpose was to create good men, trusting to their influence for the regeneration of mankind, avoiding whatever, by causing disturbance, might alienate, discourage, or divert men from self-examination and self-discipline. It was certain that the multitude cared nothing for philosophical speculation, and it was equally certain that any discussion of social themes would arouse disaffection. The field of Christian character was wide, and its elements were well understood and cordially respected. We need not, as was the fashion, impute cowardice to the resolution to shun dispute and division and pretentiousness. There was a deliberate purpose to keep clear of "exciting" subjects, a definite, systematic, reasoned exclusion of every thing that looked like an introduction of controverted topics. There was certainly a good deal to be said in favor of the policy of silence. Timidity there was assuredly, but there was also a *rationale* of conservatism, as Emerson explained. Temperament had a good deal to do with this moral quiescence; education played a large part; association was important; social position, for the clergy were at the head of the social scale, had a great influence. But the prime circumstance of all was a theory of ministerial responsibility to the profession. The Church was to them an institution, a divine institution. Its forms of observance and faith were appointed from on high. Its Christ was a Saviour; its Bible was a revelation. And while interpretations might differ as to the meaning of the creed, or the significance of the ceremonies, there they were, and their validity must be admitted by every priest. The servant must serve dutifully. He that rejects the Church must not belong to it. If one wishes to throw stones at the windows he must go outside. This, in short, was the argument. It was difficult, if not impossible, to answer, half a century or more ago. Mr. Emerson having tried in vain to widen the Church, left it for another career. George Ripley abandoned it because it did not allow of industrial experiments. Parker remained in it, though he too had virtually seceded from it, having dropped the sacraments, discarded the creed, rejected the Bible as a source of authority, deprived Jesus of his saving attributes, and shifted the centre of inspiration to another basis. His prodigious popular talent enabled him to undertake this. Of course, he was perfectly honest. His sincerity was above dispute. But his critics said that the position he held was not logical. Nor was it. His invincible force alone made it tolerable; and as they did not possess this invincible force, they could not understand it. Now all is changed; but then it could hardly be surprising if good men—the best men—postponed their private wishes and closet opinions to the overwhelming strength of the instituted religion, with its immense influence, its all but universal following, its definite hopes, clear promises, and vast benefactions. Even the largest humanities lay concealed there, if one could wait for them. So these men wrought in faith, and were patient. They did not believe in leaving their ark. Though it floated on troubled waters, it did float. It was "narrow"; it was not any too nice; still, the future of man seemed to be in it; the dove was sent out, the pledge of dry land was welcomed. This was its prayer:

> And still on life's baptizing tide
> Or sorrow's bitter sea,
> Descending Peace be multiplied
> And hallow hearts to Thee.

II.

AN EXAMPLE.

PERHAPS the class of believers here described can be best portrayed by an instance, and I choose Nathaniel Langdon Frothingham, partly because I know him better than I know others, partly because my own disposition furnishes, in some degree, a key to his, and partly because he was an unique, typical, well-known person, admirably supplied with the qualities that illustrated his companions. The family was an old one, and, in some of its branches, distinguished. It bore a coat-of-arms, a sign of gentility. The origin of the name is uncertain; it may come from "Frod-hame" (the home of the sage), or from "Fodder-hame" (the home of the man who furnishes the *fodder* for cattle), or "Foighting-hame" (the home of the warrior). In Scotland it was associated with dukes. "Fotheringay" may be the same appellation. The spelling was various, Frottinghame, Frattinghame, Flathinghame. The family was probably of Scottish descent, but the "Signiory" of Holderness in Yorkshire appears to have been its chief seat. There was Frodinghame

Hall, the residence of the feudal lords of the soil from near the Conquest until the seventeenth century. A certain Piers Frothingham married a daughter of Sir William Boynton de Sadberg, in 1250. We hear of a Sir Peter Frothingham in 1314; of Sir Peter de Frothingham, his descendant. There was a Rev. Sir William in 1503. Sir John Lister Frothingham was knighted by Charles I. The Frothinghams of Holderness attained to some opulence through mercantile operations. But none of this splendor lighted on the William Frothingham who came to New England, probably with John Winthrop in 1630; who was appointed in 1634 one of eleven Selectmen of Charlestown; and was, at first, an adherent of John Wheelwright, of Anne Hutchinson memory. This William was a sort of carpenter. The family pursued a peaceful and honest calling as cabinet-makers, joiners, carriage-builders, in the colony. Of this William, Nathaniel Langdon was a direct descendant. His father, Ebenezer, was a crockery-merchant and appraiser of taxes in Marshall's Lane, near the Boston Stone. He married Joanna Langdon,—whence the middle name. The name "Nathaniel" was common in the family, and Miss Langdon had a brother so called, which circumstance added weight at the baptism of the eldest son.

Nathaniel Langdon Frothingham was born on the twenty-third day of July, 1793. The house still stands, though somewhat altered in the course of years. Before the Frothinghams held it it was owned by Ebenezer Hancock, younger brother of the Governor, who was paymaster in the army, an office which made him very popular, especially when the treasury had something in it. The house was a comfortable brick mansion, not stylish, but in a fashionable quarter of the town, on a narrow way at some distance from the main street. Boston was then a small place, of somewhat over thirty thousand inhabitants. Faneuil Hall was standing, so was the corn-market near by, whence comes Corn Hill; but the spot which Quincy Market occupies was covered with water. The "Neck" was a neck indeed, thin and slender. Charles Street bounded the city on the west. The mansion of Governor Hancock was considered out of town. The child was too young to see the fifteen milk-white horses which drew the corner-stone of the new State-House to its place on the hill in the "Governor's Pasture," where, on the 4th of July, 1795, it was dedicated with grand masonic ceremonies, in presence of Governor Samuel Adams, Paul Revere looking on. But he might have witnessed the procession when the members of the General Court walked solemnly from the old State-House to their new lodgings in Beacon Street. For this was in 1798.

Yes, Boston was a small town territorially, but intellectually there was probably no city in the world so full of life. It was always remarkable for explosions of mind. Nor is this wonderful as we remember the character of the men who founded it, —their mental force, their education, their moral courage, their independence, their spiritual energy One of the first things they did was to found a college. In 1636 the General Court voted the sum of £400 towards the undertaking, and its influence has been steadily exerted in favor of thought. Libraries sprang up rapidly, stimulating knowledge of every kind. There was a passion for learning. There was from of old faith in reason, and faith that reason would justify reverence. Books multiplied. It is true that Noah Webster wrote ten letters to Dr. Joseph Priestley, who had criticised in a stately manner the literary services of America,—letters that were printed in a pamphlet at New Haven in 1801,—in the course of which he allowed that "our colleges are disgracefully destitute of books and philosophical apparatus"; that "scarcely a branch of science can be fully investigated in America"; that "in the higher branches of literature our learning is superficial to a shameful degree"; that "as to classical learning, history, civil and ecclesiastical, mathematics, astronomy, chemistry, botany, and natural history, excepting here and there a rare instance of a man who is eminent in some one of these branches, we may be said to have no learning at all, or a mere smattering"; that "as to libraries, we have no such thing. There are not more than three or four tolerable libraries in America, and these are extremely imperfect." And George Ticknor, in 1814, complained that "good school-books were rare in Boston, and that no copy of Euripides, in Greek, was to be found in any bookstore in New England." But this was to be expected in a country which had but few scholars, was poor, thinly peopled, and mainly devoted to industrial pursuits. And when we remember that Noah Webster was writing to a man of science, besides being captious himself, and that George Ticknor trod the upper fields of literature, there is pretty warm praise. Webster asserts that "almost all read the best English authors. . . . If you can find any country in Europe where this is done to the same extent as in New England, I am very ill informed." (" American Men of Letters, Noah Webster," p. 106.) A literary club, called the "Anthology Club," was formed in 1804, established a reading-room in 1806, was incorporated as the Boston Athenæum a little while afterwards. After two locations—one in Scollay Square, another in Tremont Street, where the building of the Historical Society now stands— it was removed to Pearl Street, to the large house presented to the corporation by James Perkins. In 1820 there were 20,000 volumes on the shelves. The library of Harvard University, which began with 300 volumes, had 72,000 in 1850, and now numbers more than 300,000. So inordinate was, from the outset, the craving for information. My father in his manhood made constant use of the Athenæum and of Harvard College library. At this time, or soon after, there were fine private collections of books : Charles F. Adams' (18,000), W. H. Prescott's (16,000), George Ticknor's (13,000), Edward Everett's (7,500). Every gentleman had books. Public schools were established early, the first one being opened in 1635. Private schools had patrons. "The teaching and maturing" of youth was immediately thought of. John Cotton, it is thought, set on foot the Latin School, having brought from old Boston, in Lincolnshire, the memory of the Free Grammar School founded by Queen Mary. When young Frothingham was ready to go, it was probably under the charge of Samuel Hunt, who took the head mastership in 1776, and remained in possession for about thirty years. The schoolbuilding then stood where the Parker House is now. Mr. Hunt was a master of the ancient type, but there is no record of young Frothingham as being an unruly lad, or any thing but a good scholar. The fact that he afterward was a tutor there is evidence of that.

From the Latin school he went, naturally, to Harvard College. Harvard Hall was at that time the centre of college life. There the professors met the pupils, there the pupils met each other; there was the library. University Hall was not built until 1815. When Frothingham entered there were three dormitories, Massachusetts Hall, Hollis, and Stoughton. The college yard was considerably smaller than it is now.

Samuel Webber, the former Professor of Mathematics, was inaugurated President of the College on May 12, 1806, but died on July 7, 1810; and John Thornton Kirkland was chosen in his place. He was inaugurated on the 14th of November, 1810, and had a distinguished administration. Early in his career attention was turned to the necessity of establishing a School of Theology in the University. The bequest of the Hon. Samuel Dexter of $5,000 for the purpose of promoting a "critical knowledge of the Holy Scriptures" was announced to the Corporation by his son about five months before Dr. Kirkland came in. In May, 1811, trustees of the Dexter Fund were appointed, and in August of the same year Joseph Stevens Buckminster was chosen Dexter Lecturer on Biblical Criticism. This remarkable step was preceded by a period of gradual change in doctrinal opinion, and led to the formation, in 1816, of "A Society for the Promotion of Theological Education in Harvard University," with this fundamental article in its constitution: "It being understood that every encouragement be given to the serious, impartial, and unbiassed investigation of Christian truth, and that no assent to the peculiarities of any denomination be required either of the Students, or Professors, or Instructors." The Society was officered as follows: John Thornton Kirkland, D. D., *President;* Samuel Parkman, Israel Thorndike, and Peter C. Brooks, *Vice-Presidents;* Francis Parkman, *Recording Secretary;* Charles Lowell, *Corresponding Secretary;* Jonathan Phillips, *Treasurer;*

James Savage *Vice-Treasurer;* Dr. Porter, Joseph Story, Josiah Bartlett, Daniel A. White, Joseph Coolidge, James Perkins, Dr. Popkin, Charles Davis, John Howe, *Directors;* Benjamin Pickman, William Prescott, James Lloyd, Josiah Quincy, Andrew Ritchie, *Trustees;* Thomas Wigglesworth, Samuel May, Israel Manson, *Auditors.* Life subscriptions, annual subscriptions, and donations supported the Society.

"Commencement" at Harvard was a great day, a public day, festive and showy. It was formerly wild, turbulent, rude, as the 4th of July was, as all holidays were; but it had become more decorous and elegant. Young Frothingham had an English oration, the subject of which was "The Cultivation of the Taste and Imagination," and which was described by Dr. Pierce as "written with purity and pronounced with elegance."

Of the career at Cambridge little is known. He was an exemplary youth, dutiful, diligent, faithful; but he did not distinguish himself until his third year, when he became eminent as a classical scholar, as a writer of pure English, as a rhetorician, the special favorite of Joseph McKean, the Professor of Oratory. His selection for the English oration on graduating and his later appointment as teacher of rhetoric and oratory at the age of nineteen are proofs of his capacity and taste. He was of the class of 1811; was but eighteen when he graduated; was preceptor for three years, studied divinity in the meantime, and was ordained minister of the First Church in Boston, in 1815. Here he remained as long as he was able to fill a pulpit, leading a literary and churchly life, devoted to parish work, secluded and laborious. The duties at Cambridge were not arduous, and it was easy to prepare for a profession which, at that time, required no outward experience of a social kind, but a large acquaintance with books and opinions. The Church was then the great opening for aspiring young men. Theology was the most tempting study. The ministry was the chosen profession. Edward Everett, Frothingham's classmate, was first a clergyman; so were Mr. Palfrey and Mr. Sparks. Advancement was through this calling. Literature clustered about it. The community honored it. It was devoted to the highest ends, those of piety, humanity, and knowledge. It was ideal in the most exalted sense. It gave the widest expansion to the mind. The Unitarian ministry, in particular, greatly owing to the influence of Dr. Kirkland and Mr. Buckminster, was the resort of aspiring souls and opened a large career. Both science and philosophy were in this country but speculations, untried and ineffectual. The English and Scotch scholars had the field, and it was undisputed. Literature was baptized into the name of religion, and learning was identical with belief in the Gospel. Criticism was confined to Germany. Infidelity had a bad name. But inside of Christianity reason was free; mind was unfettered; conscience was buoyant, energetic, humane; each had room enough. Ardent spirits found faith secure, and spirits not ardent could repose and ponder at leisure. There was no turmoil, no exciting warfare, no moral agitation. The political as well as the social horizon was unclouded. The period of anti-slavery struggle had not begun. Transcendentalism was unborn; Humanitarianism was still in the air; Rationalism, in the later objectionable sense, was unheard of. Ripley and Emerson were boys, Parker was a child, Channing had not preached his Baltimore sermon. Mr. Frothingham had been five years in the pulpit when the Unitarian controversy broke out, so guileless was the current opinion, so light was the bondage of the creed, so easy was it to "walk large" over the religious domain, changing idols into ideals, sacraments into symbols, and dogmas into sentiments. The Unitarian schism was probably inevitable, and we are bound to believe was, on the whole, beneficial to the cause of truth. But in his moments of sentimentalism one is inclined to wish that the bitterness of dispute might have been spared, that the gradual transformation of the ancient faith might have been allowed to go peacefully on. The old bottles must break under the pressure of fermentation in the new wine, but we cannot severely blame those who, wishing to preserve the well-seasoned jars, diluted the wine and prevented the fermentation. They were determined to exhaust the capacity of the beloved vessels before trying new ones, and naturally felt a tenderness for the rich skins that interfered somewhat with their liking for the wine. In fact they did not believe in the quality of the new wine, being deeply persuaded that the branch could not bear fruit itself, unless it abode in the vine, and that Christ was the vine. To doubt that, was not to be thought of. Whatever else might be questioned, this stood fast. This must be assumed as a first principle. All Christian faith was built on this, new and old alike, and although the interpretations of the Saviour's rank, mission, office, might vary as years went on, this central position remained unassailable.

III.

THE FIRST CHURCH.

The history of the First Church in Boston deserves serious study. It is the history of spiritual New England; a history of intellectual growth. I am convinced that an instructive chapter in the story of evolution might be written, showing that Transcendentalism was a legitimate product of Puritanism; that Emerson was a direct descendant of the Mathers. The sacerdotalism had long ago dropped off; the dogmatism had disappeared; but the force of the idealism persisted, and faith in the moral nature of man, which was the distinguishing feature of Emerson's teaching, rose high. The church had deep foundations. It was first organized in Charlestown by John Winthrop and his friends, in pursuance of their plan to make the Christian virtues supreme. So eager were they that they could not wait for any meeting-house, even the humblest, but gathered under a tree, thus foreshadowing Bryant's idea in regard to man's "first temples."

"The groves were God's first temples."

THE FIRST CHURCH.

On the same day, August 27, 1630, Rev. John Wilson was installed as "teacher." Next year a removal to the south side of the river took place, and, in 1632, a house of worship was erected on the south side of State Street, on the corner of Devonshire Street. It was exceedingly simple, with mud walls and thatched roof. The second meeting-house was built on Washington Street, opposite State Street, then "Cornhill Square." This was more stately, and was burned in the fire of October, 1710. The third house, erected on the same spot, and familiarly known as the "Old Brick," was dedicated on May 3, 1713. This was taken down in 1808, and, the same year, the building in Chauncy Place was put up. The "Governor's pew" in the "Old Brick" was a conspicuous object, with its curtains and its raised platform. The architecture was of the colonial period, unadorned and simple, yet cheerful too. The Chauncy Place meeting-house was altered in the summer of 1843, a flat roof of colored panes being substituted for the high ceiling, and giving rise to the witticism that Dr. Frothingham was going to try to "raise Christians under glass." Business claimed this site also, and in 1868 the new edifice at the corner of Marlborough and Berkeley streets received the society.

Mr. Frothingham was ordained, after a unanimous invitation, on the 15th of March, 1815, Dr. McKean preaching the sermon, Mr. Channing offering the prayer of consecration, Dr. John Lathrop giving the charge, Mr. Thacher making the address to the people, Dr. Henry Ware, the elder, offering the opening supplication. There was an ecclesiastical council, of course, and a dinner after the exercises at "Concert Hall." Hymns of a solemn strain were sung after the dinner, which, we may hope, was festive.

The predecessors of Mr. Frothingham were remarkable men—some of them distinguished: John Wilson, John Cotton, John Norton, John Davenport, James Allen, John Oxenbridge, Benjamin Wadsworth, Thomas Bridge, Thomas Foxcroft, Charles Chauncy, John Clarke, William Emerson, John Lovejoy Abbot. Dr. Chauncy was my father's favorite, apparently on account of his liberality and sweetness. In a discourse on occasion of the two hundredth anniversary of the church's existence, August 29, 1830, he wrote this: "With CHAUNCY a new era commenced. He viewed religion with naked human eyes, and not in unreal visions, or through the discolored and distorting medium of technical systems. He looked upon the world, and was not afraid to bind up his hopes in the common hopes of mankind. He looked up to heaven, and its throne was to him filled with the unclouded radiancy of love. He beheld the churches agitated with a storm of religious excitement, and he rebuked both the winds and the sea." Dr. Chauncy was minister from October, 1727, until February, 1787. He was not technically a Unitarian—that is, he did not deny the Trinity, but his was the religion of the heart, and he admitted the humanity, while preserving the dignity, of his profession. A curious illustration of this was his driving through the streets of Boston in an old-fashioned chaise with long shafts, and a seat for the driver where our whiffletree is. The doctor sat up straight, in a cocked hat and with a gold-headed cane, and the driver, who, in this case, was a negro boy, gave his companions, as he met them, a touch with his whip. The picture was a droll one, —the city, the vehicle, the stately parson, the small snip of a boy, the absence of rebuke. In all the history of the church there was no discussion on theological grounds, strictly. There might have been a difference of opinion, but there was no dispute about beliefs. Change in belief came gradually and almost imperceptibly. There was simply a more generous interpretation of ancient formulas. Of the least theological disaffection in the church, no record is extant.

The original covenant of the church, never disavowed or altered, is exceedingly tender, spiritual, and humane. There is no savor of dogmatism about it. Here it is:

"In the name of our Lord Jesus Christ and in obedience to His holy will and Divine ordinance.

"We whose names are hereunder written, being by His most wise and good Providence brought together into this part of America in the Bay of Massachusetts, and desirous to unite ourselves into one congregation or church, under the Lord Jesus

Christ our Head, in such faith as becometh all those whom He hath redeemed and sanctified to Himself, do hereby solemnly and religiously (as in His most holy presence) promise, and bind ourselves, to walk in all our ways according to the rule of the Gospels, and in mutual love, and respect each to the other, so far as God shall give us grace."

This Covenant was repeated, on the occasion of the installation of the present minister, the faith was reiterated, the pledge emphasized. The condition of the promise " to walk in all our ways according to the rule of the Gospels, *so far as God shall give us grace,*" proved to be quite necessary, for there ensued a sharp collision between the first incumbents when the "Antinomian Controversy" raged, and there were occasional infelicities of temper, but the purity of the faith was unbroken. The belief in the divinity of the Son of God, His special mission as Saviour of the world, and in the Bible as a direct revelation of the Supreme Will, was the traditional creed of the church which no member was at liberty to disavow. Whatever might be objected to it from outside, inside the communion every man of honor was bound by it so long as he remained; so long, that is, as his private convictions allowed him to profess it as, in the main, true. The large indefiniteness of the articles rendered it easy to interpret them liberally, and to submit private thoughts to public declarations, in the interest of brotherhood and spiritual edification. The love of Christ was constraining and inasmuch as no fetters of dogmatism were felt, the mind could range over a broad field without disloyalty.

One usage Mr. Cotton brought over from old Boston in Lincolnshire, the famous lecture which he preached every Thursday, while he was under the directions of the Bishop of Lincoln, and in relations of friendship with the Earl of the same title. It was well called "great," for great it was at first. On the very month of its establishment the Court issued an order prescribing the hour at which it should be attended, one o'clock in the day. The hour was presently changed, first to twelve o'clock, and, towards the close of the century, to eleven. This was in the time of Increase Mather, who reproved the people for their slack attendance, and declared that "it would be an omen of their not enjoying it long, if they did not amend." But in the beginning there was no tardiness. On the 4th of March, 1634, by order of court a "marcate" was erected at Boston, to be kept upon Thursday the 5th day of the week, being the lecture day." About the same time, an excommunicated person was compelled to confess, among other offences, his "sometimes forsaking the Lecture,"—for the sake of some vicious indulgence, it was surmised. At the meeting all that was most honorable was in attendance. The governor was present, the counsellors were in attendance; the magistrates, the dignitaries, the people of all conditions, from miles around. The villages sent their pastors and farmers. The college sent its officers and students. The schools dismissed their pupils, for all minor instruction must cease. The circumstance that Thursday was fixed for public executions and that the culprit had to attend on the sermon, may have had an effect in drawing a crowd. The social customs and even the dress of men and women were affected. The rules of conduct, the tenets of faith, the laws of the State felt the influence. There were rows of scarlet cloaks, and piles of artificial hair, and the bright faces of beauty. The lecture was followed by a gathering of the people, the discussion of municipal regulations, and the consideration of all matters that concerned the community.

From this high estate the institution went through several processes of decline. Its honor decreased, its attendance fell off, the cold weather sensibly diminished the audience. In the winter of 1715, during a violent snow-storm, the worshippers were so few that some curious chronicler counted but sixteen women and two hundred men. In 1830 scarcely a vestige of its ancient renown remained. During the siege of Boston, in the war of the Revolution, it was discontinued altogether, but was resumed on the deliverance of the town from the British. The officers of the American army celebrated their victory in the First Church; Washington came; there was "awful mirth." But the glory was of short continuance. The joy was rather civil than religious;

and the temple might have been closed for this ceremony then.

In my youth the Thursday Lecture was but a shade of the past. Ministers of the neighboring towns came to Boston on that day because it was convenient, and held a sort of exchange at a bookstore on Washington Street, greeting each other and arranging for Sunday, as was the custom at that period. They made the chief part of that small congregation. The magistrates were not there. The business men were not there. Fashion was not there. A few ladies—mostly aged and in black, with smelling-bottles—made a point of going, to keep up appearances. The galleries were empty; the pews were thinly peopled. The music was of that extremely simple kind which one expects from voluntary efforts: —a son of the minister of the First Church played the organ, and another son blew the bellows. The clamor for the office of preacher was feeble on the part of the brethren. The man whose turn it was regarded himself in the light of a victim. The whole performance was unreal. The ordinance flamed up for an instant when Theodore Parker occupied the pulpit, but the excitement was for that occasion only. In order to avoid any such demonstration in the future, it was determined to exclude Mr. Parker,— a process that should not have been necessary, as the man certainly had no place in the First Church. With this end in view it was, after much discussion in the Boston Association, resolved that the minister of the church should, as at first, take the service into his own hands, and invite whomever he would to help him. This was, perhaps, the best course that was open. It is true that this ancient prerogative had been virtually surrendered a hundred and sixty-five years before, but this was not of public record. It seems that in 1679, less than a generation after Mr. Cotton's death, which occurred in 1652, there was passed "an order and advice of y^e magistrates, yt all the elders of this towne might jointly carry on the 5th day lecture." This order was reluctantly accepted by the ministers in office, as appears. "In answer to y^e Hon$^{ed.}$ Magistrates about the Lecture; Tho' as an injunction wee cannot concur with it, but doe humbly bare our witness against it, as apprehending its tending to y^e infringement of Church Libertie; yet if the Lord incline the hearts of the other Teaching officers of this time to accept of y^e desire of our officers, to give ye assistance with those of this church, who shall be desired to carry on their fifth day lecture, wee are willing to accept their help therein." From that time, other ministers, as they were added to the Congregational body, and were disposed, took part in the exercises, and the original practice was discontinued.

It would not be fair, however, to impute the new departure wholly to a dislike of Mr. Parker. The Standing Committee of the church complained of the promiscuous crowd of people, the consequent dirt, the injury done to furniture, and said they could not heat the building, or ask the sexton to clean it, for such performances. This protest fell in with the desire to restore the ancient usage. The plan was pursued for some time, but the old position was never recovered. It was generally thought that the new device was aimed at "rationalism"; to be, in its intent, exclusive, and this brought it into disrepute. Mr. Parker, too, had numerous allies, who cried out against what they called persecution. Then, it was more difficult than ever, in the divided state of opinion, to find men to fill the place. Still, the plan, as I said, was persevered in. In Dr. Frothingham's diary, under date of February 8, 1849, there is this entry: "Preached the Thursday Lecture in course." Again (November 2d): "Preached ye Lecture, Mr. Robbins failing to appear." On Sunday, March 10, 1850, his farewell sermon was delivered, and the lecture lapsed for a time. Dr. Frothingham's successor, Rev. Rufus Ellis, tried to revive it in 1858, five years after his installation, and invited ministers of all denominations, not Congregationalists alone, but Episcopalians as well, Methodists, Orthodox of different names. Among others, James Freeman Clarke and J. L. Diman preached. But this arrangement did not last longer than three or four years. Then the famous lecture,—which in the Old World had started the Congregational idea, for Congregationalism seems to have grown out of this independent, popular discourse, and in the New World was closely associated with the affairs of State and society,—disappeared from view. While the edifice in Chauncy Place was yet standing, it vanished. The house on Berkeley Street never knew it. A history of the lecture down to 1833 was given in a discourse entitled "The Shade of the Past," by N. L. Frothingham. Its subsequent history may be found in Mr. Arthur B. Ellis' excellent "History of the First Church."

It should be added that no special preparation for the lecture was expected. Ministers brought sermons which they had on hand. The day was simply a gospel day, an opportunity for spiritual edification; an hour of grace between the Sundays; a link in the chain of divine ministration; an assertion that there were no purely secular seasons, that all days were the Lord's.

IV.

THE DOGMATICAL POSITION.

THIS is the place to give some account of the dogmatical and ecclesiastical relations of the Unitarians I am describing. My father, and with him all his friends, was absorbed in the endeavor to apply Christianity to personal character, taking men and women one by one and trusting to their influence for the regeneration of society. With the philosophy of religion they had no concern. Christianity was the established faith. They thought of no other. And this, I repeat, was an institution, with roots in history, and traditional beliefs, which might be modified but could not be abolished. Life was consumed in services to individual souls, rendered in public and in private. The diary has in it nothing but records of prayers with the sick, visits of consolation to the afflicted, ministrations of hope to the dying, benedictions over the dead, words of admonition or cheer for those entering upon the duties of existence. There was great diligence in sermon writing, between thirty and forty sermons a year, sometimes more, being prepared. There were journeys on evangelizing work, errands in aid of a brother, exchanges at a distance, baptizings, communions, counsellings.

The religion was essentially the old one, softened by thought, knowledge, experience, feeling; a faith rather than a creed, a sentiment more than a dogma, not sharp in outline, but full of emotion and charged with conviction, slightly illogical perhaps, but firm, —a religion of the heart. I shall give its main points in the language of my father, than which none can be more precise. This language is taken from discourses preached in the regular course of ministry, for there is no formal theological treatise. It was not his way to write such, nor the way of his friends. And if it is objected that the statements lack something of the exactness of definition that belongs to a creed, it should be remembered that the words are addressed to the spiritual nature, and aim rather to awaken the sensibilities than to satisfy the understanding. In fact, the very theory was that the religious sentiment was, not supreme only in importance, but the most valid interpreter of faith. The following is a just account of the position:

"Such is a brief statement of our leading doctrines. We hold them as important. We embrace them as precious. At the same time we openly declare that we prefer a lovely disposition, and a virtuous purpose, and a heart that is right before God and man, to any mere speculative conclusions whatever." And again:

"But it will be said, and not without reason, that this effect will hardly be produced at all, unless there are some positive doctrines, however faintly recognized, to which it stands in relation. There must be something underneath, on which conviction is built, if we would maintain it for any rational support. Even though we are not aware of it, it must be there in the substance of some divine truth. We admit that this is to some extent so, and yet we should not lose sight of the fact that faith is more of a sentiment than of a rigid rule. It is a child of the affections. While on one side it deals with arguments and evidence, and arrays itself in texts and formularies, appearing, like the wise son of David, clad 'in all his glory'; on the other hand, it unfolds itself in the responsibilities of a well-ordered nature, a spontaneous 'lily of the field,' more glorious still. And we are not apt to do justice enough to this unartificial growth. We are too fond of speculating and disputing and drawing lines of theological demarkation, instead of repairing to the great elements of religion and humanity, and considering that the same tranquil assurance may exist on both sides of any line that you can draw."

Here is his most positive assertion of the claims of credence, and his hardest speech against those who rejected Christianity as a form of belief. It is from the four discourses, "Deism or Christianity," preached in 1845 against the opinions ascribed to Theodore Parker:

"The denomination to which we belong took its origin in resistance to confessions that it could not subscribe, and a dictation to which it would not submit. The evils of ecclesiastical positiveness and tyranny have so marked themselves upon the church that every thing which reminded of them became odious. Liberal religion had to employ its energy for a long time in that direction mainly, and seemed to take the attitude rather of vindicating its freedom and protesting against what was false, than of insisting on what was vitally true. Hence occasion has been taken to say that we cannot, consistently with our own principles, draw any lines of demarkation. All this is indiscreetly spoken, whether by those who are without our body or those who are within it. . . . But why so? By rejecting the precepts of our neighbors we do not resign all precepts for ourselves. . . . If any complain of restraints on religious liberty, it will be well for them to remember that there are religious obligations also. This liberty is in no danger where we are, though many swelling vanities are uttered, and some artifices are practised, under that pretence. And if it is really so great a good let us have a portion of it too, as well as others. Surely there is a liberty of enclosure, as well as of spread. We may claim to be by ourselves so it be with a due consideration for those who differ from us. There is no harm in a simple wall of separation, and we neither commit persecution nor inflict martyrdom if we make it high enough to be seen from some distance. Men may call it exclusiveness, if they will. But every one that has a house over his head is in a sense exclusive. He does not build that he may live out-of-doors, nor could he well call it a house if it took in all that is abroad.

"Let us have a belief, therefore. How can we otherwise have any portion in the believer's rest or hope? Let us have a creed also. For how else can we tell or know what we believe? Only let it be held with humility, and seriousness, and charity. We need not ask too curiously how much there is of it, nor of what precise kind it is. We will not ask this of others at all, for it is their concern and not ours. But if their doctrine jostle or attack us, it may impose upon us an obligation to keep it aloof from our fellowship, and to give to the world a reason for the different faith that we are attached to. . . . One thing at least is as clear as the light, that the Gospel can be of service only so far as it is accredited. If it have no sanction for us, it has no comforting trust for us."

The creed itself would not have satisfied a severely critical mind. It would not have contented Abelard, though it might have pleased Emerson. It was rather rhetorical than dialectical. It would hardly have inspired St. Francis d'Assisi or Martin Luther. It was not calculated to form heroic virtues,—courage, boldness, fortitude, consecration, self-surrender, sacrifice, passionate enthusiasm, devotion to a cause deemed righteous, but it was relied on to foster the gentler qualities of trust, hope, patience, gratitude, submission, the love that casts out fear. As I said, the building up of personal character in courtesy, generosity, diligence, was the object, not the formation of correct opinions. "The rule over our own growth in temperance, sweetness, patience, cannot well be dispensed with."

In presenting the scheme of belief, I certainly do not defend it or its aims. It is my opinion that both are inadequate to explain the facts. My wish is simply to make it clear, and so do it justice. This summary, it may be added, is taken from a printed sermon, entitled "The Believer's Rest," preached in 1843, and privately circulated.

"And first, we believe in a paternal Sovereign of the world and of man. A Father as well as a King is upon the throne of the universe. Not by a blind chance, not by a stern fate, not by an arbitrary rule, is the destiny of things decreed, but by an unseen intelligence and a primeval love. Do you want any different doctrine as respects this inexpressible Being? Or do you think that you would gain any thing in clearness or justness of apprehension, or in piety of heart, by listening to metaphysical subtleties concerning His essence, or presumptuous familiarities about His counsels, or circumscriptions of His immeasurable attributes? Above all, do you think that you would gain any thing in that true reverence which awes, but does not perturb the soul; in that true love which raises us above a superstitious servility; in that true quietness which belongs to the mind that is stayed upon Him; by clouding the light of His countenance with vulgar terrors, and divesting Him of that gracious look by which alone we can recognize the Father of Spirits?

"Again, we believe in His Son Jesus Christ, well-beloved, and the manifestation of His love to the world. To us, 'There is but one God, and one Mediator between God and men, the man Christ Jesus.' So the apostle declares, and we cannot conceive of language being framed more explicit than this. We believe in Him as revealing a perfect duty and an anchor of hope, establishing with authority the truth that it is most important for men to receive, and breathing the full spirit by which the world is to be renovated, dying for our sins according to the Scriptures, and rising again the third day according to the Scriptures. We believe in Him, the divine word and wisdom, the way and the life. In all the offices that He bears towards our poor mortality; in the grandeur of His mission, the fruits of His sufferings, the victory of His death; in the example He set, in the laws He sanctified, in the immortal promises He spread; we steadily preach Him who was sent.

"We believe in the Spirit of the Lord, breathing wherever He wills, like the vital air that nourishes the creation; informing, comforting, vivifying; pleading with the conscience, purifying the affections; changing the carnal heart. We are no materialists; we do not profess to solve all mysteries with our logic. We do not presume to reject any word from on high, because it is mysterious. We do not think to confine within what some are fond of appealing to as 'natural laws,' the agency and grace of God. We hold to a faith transcending sight and absolute knowledge. We depend upon the spirit of a heavenly instruction and benediction. Can you approach any nearer to it by calling it a person instead of an influence? or by engaging in any technical refinements as to the modes of its operation?

"We believe in the Scriptures, as a holy testimony; a record of the Divine dispensations for the education and redemption of the human race; the great rule of faith and practice. We reverence their precepts, their narratives, their various utterances of knowledge and praise, and we do not revere them the less for reading them by the light of our own understandings and the aids of studious men, and interpreting them as our best judgment directs. We do not pretend to set forth any other gospel, or to look for any other deliverer, than the one there revealed."

In regard to human nature, a subject which was, at that time, agitating the Unitarian mind, the same authority enunciates the following:

"The present era seems to be that of the apotheosis of human nature. Human nature is exalted into the 'heavenly places' to acknowledge nothing above its own height. Man, who started into his first deviation from the truth by the worship of the surrounding universe, appears approaching, as his last delusion, to the worship of himself. Ah, poor worm! . . . Does he go almost as far, with his spiritual fancies, to cloud over the idea of 'the God and Father of our Lord Jesus Christ,' as the materialist with his doctrine that grovels the lowest? If he does, how much has he gained by casting down the graceful image that at least represented something divine, though it might have been modelled but out of clay? . . . Give me back the simple form of a child's credulity, rather than mislead me into any philosophical refinement, that instructs me to presume, and leaves me to perish."

This is like Wordsworth's sentiment:

> " Great God ! I 'd rather be
> A Pagan suckled in a creed outworn ;
> So might I, standing on this pleasant lea,
>   Have glimpses that would make me less forlorn ;
> Have sight of Proteus rising from the sea,
> Or hear old Triton blow his wreathèd horn."

The same sentiment but not the same idea. Here was no thought of returning to paganism, or of going outside of doctrinal Christianity. Expressions of this are frequent. Here is one. In the introduction to a translation of the first of the Elegies of Propertius, a writer in the Augustan Age of Roman poetry, Mr. Frothingham says:

"The last, which is, indeed, the leading, reason" [for presenting the version] "is the opportunity that it gives of comparing some of the purest sentiments of classical antiquity respecting the state of the dead, with those of the simplest minds that have the advantage of Christian education."

There was not then, as there is now, a disposition to construe favorably the language of the older religions. There might have been as much real knowledge, but it was still the fashion to look askance at other systems of faith—to call Mahomet an impostor, for instance—and to treat their nobler sentiments as shadowy, mere surmises, and of the fine minds too, vague hopes at the best, bright anticipations of certain illumined intelligences. As we know, the will to see often makes sight, and the will to see had not come to those men; *The Dial*, organ of the most advanced speculation, just venturing, in a tentative way, in its extracts from "ethnic scriptures," to depart from the accepted tradition. This example was not calculated to encourage these Unitarians to leave the beaten track. The Transcendentalists were their aversion. In natural religion they placed no confidence. It gave adumbrations, hopes, impressions, but no satisfactory evidence. "There is a conviction of right and wrong in the breast, but it has no tongue. Not the slightest whispers go round among the crowded thoughts of the heart. . . . All that we receive from these sources is the inference which we ourselves draw from what we see and experience. We know how dubious this will often be. But the revealed Gospel exhibits clear objects to our faith and affections. It speaks out, and its speech is with authority."

The dependence was on miracle. "Is there one here," said Mr. Frothingham, in a sermon on the "Manifestation of Christ," "who thinks he requires no miraculous evidence in support of his religious convictions, who feels satisfied with the proofs that the unaided mind can furnish for itself? I will not assail him, I will not charge him with throwing away all faith, because he is willing to receive it on slighter grounds than we trust it is built on. I will congratulate him that he feels his hope to be so sure. . . . But let us profess for ourselves, that we needed something more and have found it. We will own that we love to trace our faith further than to the self-taught dictates of a refined intellect and an elevated heart; even to the Fountain of Inspiration."

The ecclesiastical relations were very simple indeed. Under Congregationalism each church was a law to itself in forms of administration. It might even, in case there was no regular minister, choose a man from among its church members to serve as "teacher." Of course such a person was not recognized as a preacher by any other society. There was fellowship among the congregations,—communion, comity, consociation, sympathy, but no absolute allegiance. Councils might advise, recommend, lend their practical wisdom, but they could not dictate. They had no authority. There was no constraining organization as there was among Episcopalians or Presbyterians. The right of each congregation over its own individual members was disputed, as appears from the withdrawal that originated the 3d of October.[1] In 1811 there were twenty-two places of public worship in the town. In my youth there was only one Roman Catholic Church in Boston, the Cathedral of the Holy Cross, on Franklin Street, and there were not more than two priests there. Romanism had no hold on the influential people. It was not even dreaded, as is evidenced by the fact that leading Protestants were the first and largest givers to the faith whose spread they could not anticipate. Episcopacy was fashionable, but feeble. When my father was ordained, in 1815, there were but two establishments in the city—Christ Church and Trinity,—at opposite ends of the town; the one by Copp's Hill, the other in Summer Street. King's Chapel was Unitarian. St. Paul's parish was formed, chiefly from Trinity, in 1819. Traditions of Congregationalism were not only supreme but were taken to be everlastingly rooted in the genius of New England. The original Puritan commonwealth, simply adjusted to modern conditions,—retained, but shaded off,—was quietly accepted, and such departures as "independent" churches—churches independent of all denominational conventions, as well as of doctrinal pre-suppositions—were unheard of. The ancient principle of building up individual character on the Gospel basis was persisted in, and the method was that of industriously preaching the "Word."

It must be confessed that there was not much

[1] See H. A. Hill's "History of the Old South," vol. L., 175, 332, 365.

moral earnestness, as that term is usually apprehended, among these men. There was no "enthusiasm of humanity." This was hardly heard of then. Humanity was to be regenerated by supernatural means, not believed in or trusted. The arrangements of the world, including poverty, misery, crime, oppression, wrong, were of providential appointment, and were to be abolished by the slow operation of spiritual influences proceeding from personal virtue. The elect of the churches were thus the centres of power, and efforts were confined to the effectual use of the "means of grace." This may help to explain the circumstance that these men, so humane, so compassionate, so kindly, so conscientious, so tenderhearted, so generous, were no more interested in the organizations against slavery, intemperance, the disabilities of working men and women, bad legislation, evil customs. A sense of turpitude was entirely consistent with an apparent apathy which was born of a patient waiting on Providence, and a diligent employment of its prescribed remedies. Even Dr. Channing's society refused to open the meetinghouse for a eulogy on Dr. Follen, to be delivered by his friend S. J. May, the Abolitionist; and it has been asserted on authority that his congregation deserted him in the later years of his life on account of his anti-slavery views.[1] Dr. Channing himself sadly owned that the Unitarians, as a sect, were

---

[1] See "Diary of J. Q. Adams," and also the *Unitarian Review* for August, 1881, p. 151.

indifferent to the question of slavery, and when his meeting-house was refused to the eulogist of Charles Follen, doubted the efficiency of his ministry, and was disposed to think that he had poured out his soul in vain, if this was the result of his endeavors. No, the society did not go with him in any of his projects of reform. This may have been owing to "conservatism"; or to a sense of social superiority, an unwillingness to mingle with ordinary men and women; or to indifference to the subject; or to a want of human feeling; or to timidity, as it required some courage to befriend an unpopular cause. But it might have been due, in part at all events, to a conviction that kindness, charity, good-will were personal qualities entirely; that gentleness, sweetness, peacefulness, serenity were most desirable Christian virtues; that the office of the minister of religion was to create these graces of the private heart and to avoid matters that would raise up discord. This persuasion was certainly very strong, so strong that a leading Unitarian minister, an eminent, distinguished, and authoritative man, whose name carried universal influence,—I am speaking of James Walker, —would not, it was said, *vote*, lest he should be associated in the public mind with political opinions. He was a clergyman, and as such pledged to the single duty of educating people in character. As an illustration of this sentiment I may cite the words of another well-known, able, most excellent minister in the neighborhood of Boston. Speaking of the Abolitionists he said: "These men have brutalized the spirit of the community." Brutalized the spirit,—the spirit of peacefulness, of urbanity, of quietude, of pious acquiescence. This man was a gentleman of the old-fashioned Christian stamp, courteous, kind, a genuine lover of souls, good to the poor, generous, an example of the best preaching of the day; his sole deficiency being a want of that "enthusiasm of humanity" which is characteristic of the present generation. If we could have followed Dr. Channing's parishioners to their homes, we should probably have found them amiable in every domestic virtue, pure, temperate, humble, charitable in judgment, generous in alms-giving, benevolent and beneficent to their dependants, living under a strict allegiance to the "great task-master." There was a perception and a vivid one, though not a controlling one, of the iniquity of war and slavery, but the faith was that these evils must disappear in time before the spread of Christian charity. The following passage from a sermon preached in 1828 by F. W. P. Greenwood, makes both of these points clear:

> Let it not be said that there is no express precept in the Christian code against slavery or against war. There is more than an express precept against them; there is its whole spirit and purpose, its whole temper and influence. Show me a man who, in the spirit of Christianity and with the authority of its founder, can drag an unoffending fellow-creature from his country and kindred and make him his slave; or a man who, in the spirit of Christianity and with the authority of its founder, can march humbly, meekly, and forgivingly to seek

the life of his brother man in red battle, and I will grant that in these particulars I have overrated the influence of my religion, and that we must go to philosophy and reason alone for arguments and principles on the subjects of slavery and war.

It is understood that all these men were conservatives; but they were not conservative in the sense of wishing that the world would stop where it was, or that what existed was good enough. They believed in conscience; but it was their conviction that institutions embodied the moral sense of the race thus far, and that any further progress must be made gradually by the increase and spread of just ideas, not by sudden or violent convulsion. And if they had more regard for the actually organized moral sense than they had for its ideal possibilities in individual breasts, they are not to be accused of indifference to social advance; or if they made too little allowance for the power of heredity, education, surroundings, and were therefore disposed to be austere in judgment, it should not be forgotten that the science of sociology had not been discovered; or if, again, they found humanity so mixed up with other less reputable passions, like arrogance, self-assertion, conceit, as to be inseparable from them, it must be remembered that they had great fear of these low motives and aimed to repress them. On this point, again, Mr. Frothingham must be the spokesman of his order. Meeting a friend one morning in Leverett Street, near the prison, on the day fixed for the execution of a murderer, he expressed more gratification that the law was to be vindicated, and the safety of good citizens secured, than pity for the criminal; and when a noted philanthropist, called "The Prisoner's Friend," asked his attention to his chosen charity, he replied, taking out his pocket-book, "I will give you something, for evidently you need it, but I have no faith in your cause; my preference is for people who don't get into jail." In a sermon entitled "The Ruffian Released," preached in 1836, he said:

"I am at a loss to account for it,—I scarcely know on what principle of human nature it is to be explained,—this sympathy of well-meaning persons with those who have outraged every feeling of humanity by their savage force or their cold-hearted depravity. I can understand how the Jewish populace in an excited hour should demand the liberation of Barabbas; I can almost enter into the feelings of those who, in a season of great depression, should empty every convict's cell, saying, let us supplicate the holy and frowning heavens together, for we are all transgressors alike. But, in a state of society like our own, with institutions so free from abuse and so full of mercifulness, it is hard to comprehend why there should be such a feverish sensibility in favor of the abandoned, and so intense a wish for something better than the laws." Then follows a serious attempt to get at the secret of this kind of compassion, an attempt that is really touching in its earnestness and simplicity.

It would be a mistake to suppose that these men expected any supernatural interposition in behalf of equity or good-will; any "legion of angels," any coming of the Christ in clouds or in glory; that they were luxurious idlers, lying supinely on their oars. They worked; they worked hard. Their sermons were written with pains; their prayers were earnest; their visits of exhortation and condolence were constant and faithful; they practised self-denial every day; they felt meekly and continually the responsibilities of their calling as servants of religion. It was their deliberately adopted theory that the Church was of divine appointment; that all heavenly power was conveyed by it; that moral influence was imparted through its forms of doctrine and of rite; and, accepting their place in its administration, they, as Unitarian Christians, were answerable for their fidelity. They considered themselves as set for the defence of the Gospel, as they understood it, and were bound in honor to transmit it unimpaired. That there was an absence of the democratic temper is freely allowed, is claimed even. That temper, if manifest at all, which may be questioned, presented itself fully and in unattractive guise as revolutionary, disturbing, quarrelsome. Peace was essential to their philosophy. Their whole theory of life and influence and progress demanded conservatism. The stream might be rapid, but must be noiseless, in its flow. The Son of Man does not strive or cry, nor lift up his voice in the streets. I have a distinct recollection of Dr. Frothingham's discontent with the philosophy of "Les Miserables," Victor Hugo's famous novel, then just published. It seemed to imply that a change of outward conditions would effect a change of character; that the social arrangement was radically wrong; that the "paralysis of the person" was contingent on "the narrowness of the lot." And this ran counter to all his beliefs,—was, in truth, the exact reversal of them.

This was the real objection to Theodore Parker, that he made war against the tradition and pried up the foundations of authority as the Church had laid them,—the Church of Socinus as well as the Church of Calvin or Leo. If Parker could simply have shifted the basis of authority from the Bible to the Soul, without disturbing the traditions of faith, there might have been no contest in spite of his biting sarcasms. But he discredited all the external proofs of revelation.

It was a great deal simpler for the Unitarians to accept the "sensational philosophy," as it was called. They had been brought up in it. It was established, the doctrine of the best teachers and the highest eminence. It lent itself most readily to their conceptions of religion, to their ideas of God and his relations to the world. And it was supported by the ablest writers of the time in their own communion. The great name of Andrews Norton, that competent and conscientious and fearless scholar, was on their side. In his discourse on "The Latest Form of Infidelity," he said:

Of the facts on which religion is founded we can pretend to no assurance, except that derived from the testimony of God, from the Christian revelation. He who has received this testimony is a Christian; and we may ask now, as was asked by an apostle: " Who is he that overcometh the world, but he that believes that Jesus is the Son of God?"

James Martineau, too, in the " Rationale of Religious Enquiry," the third edition of which was published in 1845, expressed himself in the same strain:

Nor is there any intelligible sense in which one who thinks that the preternatural may be banished from the birth and infancy of our faith, can continue to take the name of Christian. . . . They are exposed to just animadversion, for having professed, by convulsive efforts of interpretation, to compress the memories of Christ and his Apostles into the dimensions of ordinary life, rather than admit the operation of miracle on the one hand, or aver their abandonment of Christianity on the other. (P. 72.)

Again:

Revealed religion comprises the ideas of God derived from the Bible, considered as the record of a Supernatural Providence. It is the name for the notions and feelings suggested by a line of Hebrew history, from the patriarchal age to the death of the last Apostle. (P. 77.)

This is an exact statement of the position I am attempting to portray, as a chronicler of the period. The Intuitive Philosophy, as it was called, resting the origin of religious ideas on the native beliefs of the human reason, necessarily made light of outward evidences,—prophecy, miracle, authenticity of the

Scriptures, narrative, mission, and saying of Jesus. When fairly apprehended, as by Emerson, for instance, these simply disappeared as silently as the bark fell away from a growing tree. Sometimes they were set aside, as by George Ripley, who chose another, more secular, calling. But in Parker's case there was the loud report of protest, coupled with the sting of an exasperating verbal logic. He was constitutionally unable to appreciate the traditional point of view. He was literal, direct, simple. There was no interval between his private thought and his public speech. He visited, in Tübingen, Dr. F. C. Baur, the founder of the famous school, the man who wrote the terrible articles in the *Jahrbücher*, aiming to show that the New Testament writings were not historical but doctrinal compositions, having a controversial tendency, and was surprised to find him preaching in a regular Lutheran pulpit. Baur, on his part, expressed amazement that Parker should proclaim his critical opinions on religion. They were conclusions of the study; surmises of scholarship; matters of literary concern; private speculations, not suitable for edification; questions for learning to decide, not for faith or feeling. But Parker could not understand this distinction.

He found fault with the chairman of a meeting of the Boston Association because he, a doctor of divinity, and a public teacher of Christianity, did, at the same time, in conversation declare that Strauss, if he had made a small, popular book, must have about put an end to historical Christianity; that the conflicting accounts in the four Gospels could not be reconciled; that one might have the moral spirit of Christianity and be a Christian man, while discarding the Christian beliefs; that prophecies might be true in intention though indefensible in form. Parker thought him a hypocrite, a time-server, a deceiver of the people, an empty babbler, dishonest and hollow. But this man did not pin his faith to historical, only to instituted, Christianity; the stories in the four Gospels might be reconciled as parables though inconsistent as narratives; one might be a Christian man, at least for a time, though not a Christian believer. C. A. Bartol, Parker's classmate, one who knew him well and loved him, in a sermon, preached after his death, touched this point nicely when he said:

In all sincerity he chose his career, but he had not faculty to penetrate the purpose or appraise the contents of a religious tradition. He understood not, in its Christian application, the solidarity of a common sentiment or the continuous and indissoluble unity of the human soul. He could do nothing with enduring institutions and operative principles in the life of mankind but analyze them and reduce them to ashes in the crucible of a speculative brain. He had no imagination, simple reverence, and holy wonder to admit marvels at which, on the road of investigation, the scientific understanding balks, but which are welcome to the higher reason in every artist and true spiritualist, to poet and painter and genius of all sorts, treading on the mysterious border, none ever measured, of the unseen world.

I must affirm the position a false one; however the man was true.

It is needless to say that this implies an intellectual limitation merely, and that in a single direction only. Mr. Parker's other mental qualities were as remarkable as his moral qualities were, and they must have been extraordinary indeed to have extorted as they did such warm expressions of regard and affection from his adversaries. Even the provocations of his manner could not alienate his opponents. The sharpest criticism ended in words of personal love.

It was probably this dread of a disorganizing tendency that alienated the first minds in the Unitarian body from transcendentalism, even when it was represented by so persuasive and lofty a spirit as that of Emerson. Not a syllable in dispraise of him was ever uttered in my hearing. His faith, his aspiration, his sweetness, his humility, his enthusiasm of spirituality, his catholicity of sentiment, his sincere demand that others should be true to themselves, his utter refusal to impose his individuality upon others, was admitted; but his philosophy, it was feared, encouraged conceit, pretension, self-assertion, and led to disintegration. He himself knew this, felt it, and tried to correct the tendency. His appreciation of mental sincerity was absolute. He cordially invited my father to the meeting at his house in Concord which resulted in the "Transcendental Club," and the offishness of the latter, who distrusted the movement, did not chill his regard, as the following entry in his "Journal" shows:

August, 1857.

I had a letter from Dr. Frothingham to-day. The sight of that man's handwriting is Parnassian. Nothing vulgar is connected with his name, but on the contrary every remembrance of wit and learning and contempt of cant. In our Olympic games we love his fame. But that fame was bought by many years of steady rejection of all that is popular with our society, and a persevering study of books which none else reads, and which he can convert to no temporary purpose. There is a scholar doing a scholar's office.

About the same time Thomas Carlyle wrote a letter to Mr. Emerson containing the following passage, which Mr. Emerson sent to my father:

By the bye, speaking of dull publics, I ought to say that I have seen a Review of myself in the *Christian Examiner* (I think that is it, of Boston); the author of which, if you know him, I desire you to thank on my part. For if a dull million is good, then withal a seeing unit or two is also good. This man images forth a beautiful idealized clothes philosopher, very satisfactory to look upon; in whose beatified features I did verily detect more similitude to what I myself meant to be than in any or all the other criticisms I have yet seen written of me; that a man see himself reflected from the soul of his brother man in this brotherly improved way is one of the most legitimate joys of existence.

Reference is here made to an article on "Sartor Resartus" in the *Christian Examiner* for September, 1836, by N. L. Frothingham. Both tribute and review are the more remarkable that Mr. Frothingham was not an admirer of Mr. Carlyle's later ideas in politics, philosophy, or religion; but he had a real enthusiasm for eloquent language, and a love of fresh, wild, independent speculation; and when the purely literary taste could act freely, untrammelled by dogmatic considerations, as was not always the case, he was exceedingly generous.

In order to make the ecclesiastical position perfectly intelligible, it is necessary to say something about James Freeman Clarke's scheme for a free society. In his early years Mr. Clarke glorified the West, spoke disrespectfully, to put the case mildly, of New England Unitarianism, and criticised rather roughly some of its leading men. On his return from Louisville in May, 1840, a return to the East which was severely commented on in Boston, he established there, in 1841, the "Church of the Disciples," an organization that embodied three principles: "a free church; a social church; and a church in which the members, as well as the pastor, should take part." None of these ideas were popular in New England, in fact they were against all its habits and especially repugnant to the Unitarians I am concerned with, as well on the score of its voluntaryism and its sociability as on the ground of its democracy. It is not surprising, therefore, that the venture should be looked at askance; that in view of his encroachment on old-established relations, Mr. Clarke should be charged with displaying "a piratical flag"; that, coming back from the installation in Freeman Place Chapel, in March, 1848, my father, one of the aggrieved ones, should have remarked that

"David's soul did not rejoice that day." Mr. Clarke's devotion to intellectual liberty, as evidenced by his exchange with Theodore Parker in 1845, as a devout, honest Christian man who was entitled to fellowship, did not tend to increase the regard in his favor, notwithstanding his friendly disposition, his warmheartedness, his benevolence, his determination to take no offence, his official consecration to duty, his orthodoxy of opinion, his allegiance to the Christian creed. The smallest concession to the secular spirit was resented. Christianity was not, in Unitarian view, a moral, but also a doctrinal system, and any attempt to weaken that, as Mr. Clarke's plan did, as much as Mr. Parker's, though in a different way, was subversive of the Church as an institution resting on authority, and implying the imbecility of man. There was no social intimacy in Unitarian churches, for the simple reason that the people were present as *recipients*, not as *bestowers* of faith, the very "church members" being regarded as those who aspired, rather than as those who had attained. The "congregation" was simply a "distant fold," to be cared for by the shepherd, whose "drowsy tinklings" often "lulled" them, but who had better sleep than be absent.

It should be borne in mind that the social feeling with which we are familiar, which prevails in our Unitarian and in many other churches, was then a complete novelty. There was no social intercourse between members of the same religious society.

There were no parlors or kitchens or gathering rooms in church buildings. In the structure on Chauncy Place the Sunday-school occupied a room in the cellar where hogsheads of tobacco were stored. The preaching of the "Word" was the great thing, and this was for adult minds that had no other concern than for spiritual matters. As for the remaining principles of Mr. Clarke,—the free seats instead of owned or rented pews, and the participation of the laity in the administration of religion,—they never struck root into the soil of New England. Complaint was made that under the voluntary system the burden of expense fell on the few; and it is not easy to see how a clerical order can be maintained if laymen are expected to take part in the services of the Church. It is but fair to presume that these dangers were foreseen, that an honest desire to preserve the integrity of the existing state of things was, in the main, influential in deciding the action of the ministers. Merely personal considerations could not have controlled them; for no characters could have been more engaging than those of Theodore Parker, Ralph Waldo Emerson, and James Freeman Clarke.

In a brick building on Berry Street, used as a vestry by the Federal Street Church, Dr. Channing instituted, in the spring of 1820, the Berry Street Conference of Ministers, and delivered the first address on the point, "How Far is Reason to be Used in Explaining Revelation?" In this essay, which exhibited the moral issue between the Liberals and the Orthodox, he affirmed the primitive elements of all knowledge, the conception of goodness, and the conditions of truth. This, the earliest Unitarian organization, is still extant, and is, as at first, an occasion for considering the needs and prospects of the Unitarian faith. There is a "Concio ad clerum," followed by a discussion of a very frank description. The meetings were quite private; they were not advertised; no reporter was present; few, almost none beside ministers attended, as the questions raised were not supposed to interest others. It was never known what was to be said; consequently there was no general curiosity. The matters presented concerned the denomination, and the discussions turned on subjects of religious belief and parochial conduct. The introduction of the slavery issue by John Pierpont, and, later, of rationalistic criticism by Theodore Parker, interrupted the placid monotony of the exercises; but these episodes being ended, the same quiet flow went on, the steady progress of the sect in " Liberalism " affording sufficient excitement to keep minds alert.

The American Unitarian Association was formed in 1825. This, too, was the result of an invitation sent to ministers and laymen to meet in Dr. Channing's vestry for the purpose of conferring together "on the expediency of appointing an annual meeting for the purpose of union, sympathy, and co-operation in the cause of Christian truth and Christian charity."

Men like Henry Ware, Jr., James Walker, Samuel Barrett, Lewis Tappan, and Ezra Stiles Gannett were on the executive committee. The aim was not sectarian, but it was an effort to render the faith operative, a "desire to promote the increase of religion in the land." The name was chosen to avoid equivocation on the one hand, and misapprehension on the other.

The Benevolent Fraternity of Churches for the Support of the Ministry-at-Large was founded in 1834. "The sole object was to provide instruction and solace for souls, not to add another to the eleemosynary institutions of the city." This grew out of the devoted and successful labors of Dr. Tuckerman, Charles Barnard, and Frederick T. Gray. Nine parishes entered into the scheme of extending and placing on a firm foundation their work of spiritual benevolence. Ministers were supported; chapels were built, and an immense deal of good was accomplished, of a moral and religious, but also of an industrial character. At present nine churches contribute $7,362.64—Arlington Street Church, King's Chapel, Church of the Unity, First Church, West Church, Second Church, South Congregational Church, Morgan Chapel, First Parish of Dorchester. There is no assessment. There are five chapels,— Bulfinch Street, New South, Parmenter Street, Unity, Morgan. The several funds yield $279,327.72. The current expenses for 1888-9 were $19,186.33. The chapels do a vast amount of work of an educational description. They are centres of spiritual power of a large kind. And this was one only of several philanthropic missions of similar intent. The Boston Port Society was incorporated in 1829; the Seaman's Aid Society was formed in 1832; the Young Men's Christian Union was organized in 1851; the Society for the Relief of Aged and Destitute Clergymen was established in 1848. These all had a humane motive, and bear witness to the effort to raise men and women in the scale of rational beings. The working of these institutions, their machinery, so to speak, fell into the hands of a few zealous, fervid brethren, who were interested in all kinds of moral elevation, and had faith in the principle of the spiritual power latent in the individual will. The result justified such faith when it assumed an energetic form. The leaders acted on this presumption and labored with much assiduity at attempts to put their theory into operation. And yet, but for a few, the projects would have got no footing. Among those who served actively on the executive committees of the reform societies mentioned, I do not find the names of Parkman or Young or Lowell or Frothingham or Greenwood, though they all sympathized with the humane objects of the organizations, and were ready to help them forward by their influence and assistance. The truth is there was little or no denominational feeling in these men. They were Unitarians indeed in as far as they rejected the current interpretations of Scripture, and the popular doctrine of the creed, but they did not sieze upon the essential difference in idea between Liberalism and Orthodoxy, which was well stated by Channing as consisting in the validity of natural reason and conscience. In a sermon preached in March, 1835, the twentieth anniversary of his settlement in the First Church, my father said: "This is known by the name of the Unitarian controversy; and in so naming it I believe that I am giving utterance, for the first time in this desk, to that party word. This alone is saying not a little in illustration of the spirit with which the offices of religion have been here conducted. . . . We remained almost at rest in that earthquake of schism. . . . We silently assumed the ground, or rather found ourselves standing upon it, that there was no warrant in the Scriptures for the idea of a threefold personality in the divine nature; or for that of atonement, according to the popular understanding of that word; or for that of man's total corruption and inability; or for that of an eternity of woe adjudged as the punishment of earthly offences; or indeed for any of the peculiar articles in that scheme of faith which went under the name of the Genevan reformer. . . . We have made more account of the religious sentiment than of theological opinions." Elsewhere he declares: "We have a doctrine; though we are not anxious to define it over-closely nor to mark the deviation from any formulary that any may have prescribed. . . . We have been unwilling to take part in enterprises that have found unbounded favor with a large number of our friends"; an evident allusion to Unitarian activities. And again, in the address to the Alumni of Cambridge Divinity School, July 12, 1844, a discourse devoted to the maintenance of an old-fashioned policy, he said : "I have been led to choose that (theme) of the posture of our religious times; if, indeed, that can be called a posture which is never in repose"; a statement that betrays a conviction of the steady, uniform progress of religious truth, a persuasion that there has been no crisis of change, the introduction of no new principle, nothing to justify a departure from the ancient ways, in the direction of either truth or beneficence. That he stood alone in such an attitude is not to be supposed. There is no evidence that many did not sympathize with him; some, we know, did; and the position was entirely defensible on the ground of an even advance of human reason and the sufficiency of the wonted method of Christian virtue to satisfy every reasonable demand of piety. The necessity for distinction or separation was not felt; and so long as it was not, no emphasis of doctrine, organization, or action was required. In fact division was to be deprecated, and all attempts to break in upon the established order were to be deplored as useless and harmful innovation.

This account of Unitarianism is accepted by Dr. Lothrop, who writes thus in his "Reminiscences" (page 202):

From the time of Dr. Freeman's settlement at King's Chapel and the secession of the society from the Episcopal Church—all through the close of the last century and for the first forty years of this—the Unitarians were a distinct body, planting themselves upon the Scriptures as the rule and basis of faith, claiming to differ from other Christians, not on the ground of reason and philosophy, but on the interpretation of Scripture. They always distinctly acknowledge the authority of Christ as a divine messenger and teacher whose words were the supreme law in the spiritual world of religious thought and life.

He says that Mr. Parker "introduced discord into the Unitarian body."

Orville Dewey takes a broader view. In an article on Unitarianism, written for Johnson's Encyclopædia, he speaks thus:

In short, the stand taken by Unitarianism is for nature, for human nature, for every thing that God has made, as the manifestation of His will as truly as any thing written in the Bible.

But this was written in 1877, and Dr. Dewey was a forward-looking man.

The breaking up of the old theology began very soon in Massachusetts. As early as 1697 Increase Mather speaks of "miserable confusions and divisions" not only in Boston, but in Watertown, Cambridge, and Charlestown. The writer had attended a council of four churches at Watertown, where it was intended to ordain two ministers, but because of dissensions in the church there was no ordination the "like not known in New England." (See Doyle's "English Colonies in America," vol. iii., page 377.)

Still, it must be said, the Unitarians, laymen and clergymen, regarded their position as final. They could see nothing beyond but utter disbelief. Theirs was the honest conviction that development could go no further.

V.

LITERATURE AND RELIGION.

It is not at all surprising that these gentlemen felt secure in their doctrinal and ecclesiastical position. The opposition was not strong. Mr. Emerson, by far the most important dissident, sang his own song, and cast no reflections on those who were not in unison with him. Parker's assault was formidable, but was so much complicated with personal issues as to add to the confidence of his adversaries rather than to diminish it. The new philosophy seemed visionary and far off, a mist in the air, an almost inaudible note in a symphony. German criticism had not affected learned opinion to any extent. A few men were acquainted with Semler, Paulus, Strauss, De Wette, Rosenmuller, Eichhorn, Herder, but a few only. German rationalism had a bad name. Schleiermacher was a "veil-maker," Strauss a "man of straw," and it did not matter what Matter thought about gnosticism. The great scholar—Andrews Norton—thorough, careful, exact, a sceptic in the true sense of the word—that is, a scrutinizer, one who would take nothing on trust but would see things for himself before he believed in them—had been all round the sheepfold with hammer and hatchet, had tested every part, and removed the unsound portions, and was prepared to guarantee the security of each board and bolt; so great was his influence that some even fancied that he originated Unitarianism, which was a mistake. But he was a high authority. There was at that time great interest in the evidence of Christianity, in biblical criticism, and sacred learning. James Walker spoke of Mr. Norton's "great work on the genuineness of the Gospels," and Andrew P. Peabody, also one of his pupils in the divinity school, writes of him thus.*

He carried to the investigations of the sacred writings the same microscopic scrutiny and uncompromising excision of whatever can be otherwise than genuine, which the great German scholars have brought to the study of the Greek and Roman classics. . . . In the Gospels he rejected every passage, every text, every word, in which he could discover any possible token of interpolation or error in transcription ; and the books thus expurgated he received, because he had convinced himself, by research and reasoning, that they were the veritable writings of the men whose names they bear, and the authentic record of Him whose life they portray. . . . I have never known a firmer belief than his in the divine mission and authority of Jesus Christ.

Thus fortified there could be no misgiving. The mind was free to range over the whole field of literature, scientific, historical, biographical, linguistic,

* "Reminiscences," p. 74.

archæological, poetical, didactic, dramatic, miscellaneous. Almost every Unitarian clergyman had some pursuit outside of his profession. Norton was a poet, read Shakespeare impressively, edited, in connection with Charles Folsom, *The Select Journal of Foreign Periodical Literature*, republished the verses of Mrs. Hemans. Palfrey busied himself with the chronicles of New England. Young was interested in the elegant letters of the old country. W. B. O. Peabody was a student of natural history, and by appointment of the Legislature of Massachusetts wrote a report on the birds of the Commonwealth. Lunt, beside writing on subjects of biography and history, possessed poetical talents. Greenwood was devoted to the contemplation of the stars, the flowers, and every object of beauty in creation. Francis read all the new books. Walker was learned in intellectual philosophy. Hedge was an adept in history, in German literature, and many other things. Robbins disported himself in biography, with excursions in Hindu lore. In Mr. Frothingham's "Metrical Pieces" there are translations from Aratus, Propertius, Martial, Manzoni, Goethe, Schiller, Herder, Rückert, Uhland, Von Zedlitz, Von Auersperg, Heine. The hymns with which he enriched the language turn, of course, on sacred themes, abound in imagery drawn from the Scriptures, and are full of religious sentiment, but they evince a most careful regard for rhythmic expression.

There was very little interest in denominational distinctions. The term "liberal Christian" was especially repudiated as arrogant. To insinuate that others are illiberal is certainly a strange way of proving one's generosity. "The true liberal Christian," wrote Mr. Frothingham, "is he who can, in the first place, believe he may be wrong while firmly convinced he is right." The word "Christian" was more emphasized than the word "liberal." To be liberal outside of Christianity was not thought of, and inside of it liberality consisted in the willingness to receive such new truth as might break out of God's word. None were liberal in any other sense, and in *this* sense the Unitarians could not claim to be alone, nor did the wisest of them. It was in taking a poetical instead of a dogmatical view of the biblical statements that the best minds emancipated themselves from theological trammels and prepared the way for a bolder advance into the domain of universal religion. There is a curious illustration of this in an article on "Man before Adam" in the *Christian Examiner* for January, 1851. In that paper N. L. Frothingham said: "We hear it constantly with new wonder, though repeated for the hundredth time, how the true theory of the solar system was rejected as an error and persecuted as a blasphemy, because the Book of Joshua quotes from the Book of Jasher—which might have been a collection of heroic ballads, or a lyric on the 'Conquest of Canaan'—the poetical extravagance of the Hebrew captain stopping the sun, which stopping could not have been done, unless the sun moved. This ludicrous example is still a fair warning against pressing our construction of any passage of history from the elder times and the twilight of humanity, so as to bar the way of philosophic inquiry in pursuing its legitimate and peculiar researches. We may observe in passing that parallels to that passage from the Book of Jasher occur in Grecian poetry." Then he cites Homer's "Iliad" and Callimachus' "Hymn to Diana." Again, in the opening discourse of the "Sermons of a Twelvemonth," printed in 1852, Mr. Frothingham says, preaching from 1 Samuel xi., 14: "It would be ill-suited to an occasion like this, to be retracing the faint lines of a perished antiquity. What to us is Samuel, the gray-haired prophet of an infant nation, or Gilgal, a spot of ground once sacred but now forgotten, by the river of a distant land? What to us is the renewing of a kingdom that so soon and so ingloriously went to decay?"

The feeling toward science was most cordial, but, it will be observed, was confined, of necessity, to questions raised at that time. The lines were not drawn so closely then as they have been since. Darwin had not agitated the minds of that age. Still, as far as could be gone, perfect liberty was guaranteed, and on grounds entirely rational. In the article just quoted I find the following passage:

"We say, that in no case whatever, and in no degree whatever, should the student of physical science be checked or limited in his inquiries by the supposed authority of any ancient writing, however sacred. The provinces of biblical criticism and of any such science are entirely distinct from one another. It is difficult to suppose that any authentic history could travel down to us from so far; and we do not see why the Old Testament Scriptures should be set up as the arbitrator on the method of the origin of the human race as a scientific fact, any more than upon a question of geology or astronomy."

And this is called a truism to be apologized for on account of its triteness.

The literary era was introduced by Rev. Joseph Stevens Buckminster, a remarkable man, one of the most active members of the Anthology Club, a literary society which concentrated the talent of Boston and vicinity and supported the *Monthly Anthology*, a magazine chiefly literary, but instrumental also in applying the intellectual method to the problems of theology. Mr. Buckminster travelled in Europe, saw a great many distinguished men, made the acquaintance of German theology (it is said that he first introduced Marsh's translation of Michaelis into the United States), was an accomplished man of letters, had a fine library, the largest in this neighborhood, public libraries not being excepted, particularly rich in sacred and in classical books; was one of the first to institute in this part of the country the study of bibliography, and, by his own enthusiasm, lent a powerful impulse to scholarship. The systematic study of biblical criticism owed much to him and went hand in hand with learning. His father, seeing his literary bent, strongly advised him not to enter upon the clerical profession, but a predilection for that calling prevailed, and, after all, as a learned pursuit, it offered the largest scope to the mind. His early death was an immense loss to our intellectual world, at that time just starting on its career and trying to shake off the incubus of doctrinal tradition. His cultivation of ancient history, philosophy, art, even of music; his elegance of taste, his love of chaste language and harmonious sentences, rendered his influence almost poetical and truly rational, at once conservative in sentiment and progressive in thought. It is somewhat remarkable that his two successors, Edward Everett and John Gorham Palfrey, should both have left the ministry for secular pursuits. This would seem to show an overwhelming tendency toward literature. Mr. Buckminster's extraordinary charm of manner and immense popularity assisted in domesticating literature in the community and associating religion with it.

At all events, whether this was the cause or some other, a very mild type of religious doctrine prevailed among the Unitarians after Mr. Buckminster's time; after 1812 orthodoxy was transfigured.

As I read of those days I am reminded of the bronze monuments in the old world made of cannon which once belched forth flames and hot iron but now stand in mute beauty in some crowded square, gladdening the sunny space; or the threatening clouds on Mt. Washington, that melted away in the morning's beam and crept meekly up the mountain side, as if to get off under the innocent guise of a flock of sheep. Poems of William H. Furness, of Robert C. Waterston, of William P. Lunt, of John Pierpont, of Andrews Norton, of Frederic H. Hedge, of James F. Clarke, of Edmund H. Sears, of William Newell, of Stephen G. Bulfinch, and of many others, laymen as well as clergymen, are evidence of the transformation. They are sacred songs. The best of N. L. Frothingham's pieces have this shadowy background of religious sentiment, and he liked nothing that did not show it, though it must not be too conspicuous. Then he had a strong distaste for Thackeray, whom he thought worldly and flippant; and for Goethe, who was too much of a pagan for him. On the other hand, he could not bear Mrs. Browning, who seemed to him saponaceous. He required moral fibre, and, on this account, despised Coleridge, who, in his judgment, was not only selfish but pretentious, and willing to shine in borrowed plumage. Scott, and Southey, and Schiller were favorites with him; but Shelley, Byron, Heine! The more philosophic schools—Wordsworth, for example—he did not care for. He was a realist, but with a strong flavor of romanticism. The least suspicion of hollowness or cynicism he resented, and he was perhaps too ready to suspect them when they did not exist. But to return to his own verses. The following are good specimens of what I mean, and may serve as illustrations.

STRENGTH.

TO A FRIEND NEAR DEATH.

"When I am weak, I'm strong,"
    The great Apostle cried.
The strength, that did not to the earth belong,
    The might of Heaven supplied.

"When I am weak, I'm strong";—
    Blind Milton caught that strain,
And flung its victory o'er the ills that throng
    Round Age, and Want, and Pain.

"When I am weak, I'm strong,'
    Each Christian heart repeats;
These words will tune its feeblest breath to song,
    And fire its languid beats.

"When I am weak, I'm strong";—
    That saying is for you,
Dear friend, and well it may become your tongue,
    Whose soul has found it true.

O Holy Strength! whose ground
    Is in the heavenly land;
And whose supporting help alone is found
    In God's immortal hand.

O blessed! that appears
    When fleshly aids are spent;
And girds the mind, when most it faints and fears,
    With trust and sweet content.

It bids us cast aside
    All thoughts of lesser powers;
Give up all hopes from changing time and tide,
    And all vain will of ours.

We have but to confess
    That there's but one retreat;
And meekly lay each need and each distress
    Down at the Sovereign Feet;—

Then, then it fills the place
    Of all we hoped to do ;
And sunken Nature triumphs in the Grace
    That bears us up and through.

A better glow than health
    Flushes the cheek and brow ;
The heart is stout with store of nameless wealth ;—
    We can do all things now.

No less sufficience seek ;
    All counsel less is wrong ;
The whole world's force is poor, and mean, and weak ;—
    " When I am weak, I 'm strong."

A DEPARTURE.

"WEEP NOT ; SHE IS NOT DEAD."

No ! call it not to die, to pass away
Thus, and to be translated ;—every power
Of mind and spirit kept till life's last breath ;
No pain to rack the frame ; no weak regret
Or anxious doubt to cloud the parting soul ;
Peace in the heart, and hope upon the brow,—
Ay, more than hope,—faith changing into vision,
As this bright world, with all its bloom upon it,
Was opening upward into views of heaven.
This is not death, but ceasing to be mortal.
It may remind us of those old departures,
Those exoduses, told in Holy Writ,
Which that word "dead" was not allowed to darken.
" And Enoch walked with God ; and he was not,
For God had taken him."—" And he was not,"—
Not on the earth, where he had walked so long,—
As many years as each year shines in days,—
But lost to human eyesight ; disappearing
Within the splendor where he walks for ever.

When Israel's prophet, he that was its chariot
And horseman, felt that his last hour was come,—
His last below,—a fiery car and steeds
Of fire his fervid spirit snatched away.
It was not so with her. No troubled sky,
No shapes of terrible beauty, broke the calm,
That blessed her sweet translation from the world.
O mourn not for her! Mourn but for the dead,—
The dead in sins, the dead in hopelessness.
She has but just put on her incorruption.

A MEDITATION.

Too far from thee, O Lord!
The world is close upon each captured sense;
The heart's dear idols never vanish hence;
Life's care and labor still are pressing nigh;
Its fates and passions hard about me lie;—
But Thou art dim behind thine infinite sky,
    O distantly adored!

O Lord, too far from thee!
Unwingèd Time stands ever in my sight,
Flooding the Past and Now with gloom and light;
Silent, but busy, constant at my side,
It shreds away strength, beauty, joy, and pride.
Eternal! why am I from Thee so wide,
    Nor thy near Presence see?

Ne'er languished for as now.
Now that the hold of Earth feels poor and frail,—
Now that the cheek of Hope looks thin and pale,
And forms of buried love rise ghostly round,
And dark thoughts struggle on o'er broken ground,—
Where is thy face, O Father! radiant found
    With mercy on thy brow?

I know that not from far,
Not from abroad, this presence is revealed,—
To our will denied, and from our wit concealed.
No search can find Thee, no entreaty bring,—
Reason a weak, Desert a spotted thing.
O Spirit, lift me on thy dove-like wing
    To realms that last and Are!

"ARISE AND EAT."

"Arise and eat, because the journey is too great for thee."—1 Kings xix. 7.

"The journey is too great for thee,"
  The prophet heard ;
And all may list in secrecy
  The self-same word.

Life's way and work lie forward spread
  In Duty's sight ;
And who but needs more strength to stead,
  And fuller light ?

And grant no lack of view or force,—
  We faint in will ;
And so the sweep of that great course
  We fail to fill.

The weary tracts of pain and grief
  Will stretch far through,
Till the flesh sinks beyond relief,
  And the heart too.

The tangled paths of many a care
  Wind slow about ;
And straight in front, lo ! flinty fare
  And foggy doubt ;

And hindrances the firmest tread
  Will oft beset ;
And perils with a deeper dread
  The dear life threat.

"The journey is too great for thee ! "
  Beyond the bounds
Where Time parts from Immensity
  Its measured grounds.

Oh, then that other word attend !
  Its offer meet ;—
The calling of an angel-friend :
  " Arise and eat."

Eat of the fruits of holy trust
    In heavenly good ;
Not grown of dust, to mould to dust,
    But angel's food.

That food shall nerve both limb and heart
    When faint with fear ;
And pour through each immortal part
    Its power and cheer.

Thus, girt with zeal, the travelling soul,
    With patience shod,
Arrives at Horeb's distant goal,
    The mount of God.

"THINE EYES SHALL SEE THE KING."

" Thine eyes shall see the King in his beauty,
And the land that is very far off."—Isaiah xxxiii. **17.**

Stand thou but clad and begirt for thy duty
    Till all vestures of Time thou must doff ;
Then thine eyes shall see the King in his beauty,
    And the land that is very far off.

Not "they shall see the King in his glory,"—
    'T were more than those eyes might abide ;
His face bears the touch of a mortal story,
    And 't was love that scarred his side.

As far away from thought as appearance
    Lie the scenes of that prophet clime ;
Behind these mountains of interference,
    Beyond these rivers of Time.

We wander in error and weakness and vanity,
    No courage to move, and no patience to stand :
When shall we see that King of humanity,
    And tread his invisible land?

Now, in the broad high places of Feeling ;
    Now, in kind, self-forgetting Deeds,—
There lie the realms of the Spirit's revealing ;
    This is the lesson the Spirit reads.

IN BEHALF OF "THE HOME FOR DESTITUTE AND INCURABLE WOMEN."

Incurable! Sweet Nature's healing forces
  Struck at the root, and wasted at the spring;
While Art and Science, with their grand resources,
  No means can study out, no rescue bring.

Incurable! The fatal word is spoken
  That smites the faint heart with its flat despair;
Yet it is heard with spirit not all broken,
  If Gratitude and Faith their solace bear.

Waken that thankfulness in Misery's daughters,
  Which, more than expectation, holds us up;
Direct the flow of ever-living waters
  To fill the hollow of their earthen cup.

—Nature and flesh, in sinking, do not alter
  The thoughts that rise beyond decay and pain;
And, when the leech's cunning fingers falter,
  Eternal hands the inward life sustain.

Sharp the distress, as desperate the condition,
  Of those who here lie at the Beautiful Gate,
And from the name of Him, the Great Physician,
  With patient eyes their whole deliverance wait.

That name is Mercy. Show your portion of it:
  Aid your poor sisters in their sorest need;
And so join with Apostle and with Prophet,
  Who bore its message and fulfilled its deed.

Small is their hope but in the upper dwelling;
  Too weak to labor, and too lame to roam:
Let not the record that 's on high be telling
  You grudged the weary feet a transient "Home."

THE CROSSED SWORDS.

Read at a meeting of the Massachusetts Historical Society, April 28, 1859, on occasion of the transfer of two swords, so arranged, from the library of William H. Prescott to that of the Society. One of them was worn by

Colonel William Prescott at the battle of Bunker Hill ; the other by Captain Linzee, who commanded the British sloop-of-war *Falcon*, which cannonaded the American troops during that action. The two families were afterwards allied in intermarriage.

> Swords crossed, but not in strife !
> The chiefs who drew them, parted by the space
> Of two proud countries' quarrel, face to face
> Ne'er stood, for death or life.
>
> Swords crossed, that never met
> While nerve was in the hands that wielded them ;
> Hands better destined a fair family stem
> On these free shores to set.
>
> Kept crossed by gentlest bands !
> Emblems no more of battle, but of peace ;
> And proofs how loves can grow and wars can cease,
> Their once stern symbol stands.
>
> It smiled first on the array
> Of marshalled books and friendliest companies ;
> And here, a history among histories,
> It still shall smile alway.
>
> See that thou memory keep
> Of him the first Commander, and that other
> The stainless Judge,[1] and him our peerless brother,—
> All fallen now to sleep.
>
> Yet more : a lesson teach,
> To cheer the patriot soldier in his course,
> That Right shall triumph still o'er insolent Force :
> That be your silent speech.
>
> Oh, be prophetic, too !
> And may those nations twain, as sign and seal
> Of endless amity, hang up their steel,
> As we these weapons do.
>
> The archives of the past,
> So smeared with blots of hate and bloody wrong,
> Pining for peace, and sick to wait so long,
> Hail this meek cross at last.

[1] Judge William Prescott, father of the historian.

A SONNET.

How blest this peaceful hour and tranquil soul !
Why are we so disquieted in vain ?
Feeble affronts will break the temper's rein,
And little crosses master self-control.
A vanishing spark we turn to burning coal,
And insect buzzings overthrow the brain.
We fret at Time and Nature ; and complain
That fates are fixtures, and that fortunes roll.
We sigh along the past, that now is not ;
And tremble at the future, that as yet
Is nothing but what fancy's fears beget,
And draws no blade across a single spot.
Take lessons from these moments, O fond heart !
When no griefs press thee, and no terrors start.

BARTIMÆUS.

"What wouldst thou I should do for thee ?"
Said he who held the wonder-key
Of Nature's secret virtues ; who
The utmost that he said could do ;
For, not like these poor breaths of ours,
His words were gifts and acts and powers.

The questioned man had ears to hear,
And Touch was true in its small sphere ;
His tongue was quick ; he rose to meet
The Grace that called him to his feet.
But hidden were Christ's form and face,
The moving crowd, the unmoving place ;
The kingly sense that lights the mind
Was gone : Timæus' son was blind.
He answered,—did he answer right ?—
"Lord, that I might receive my sight."

Oh, chide not that he could not lift
His heart to any higher gift ;
And when a heavenly offerer came,
No heavenly gift could think or name.
"Receive thy sight," the Christ replied ;
And the glad wretch walked justified.

Sat there that day a king at hand,
With sceptre over sea and land,
And wealth and splendor round his throne,
Free to all eyes,—denied his own,—
On his crowned brow were blot like that,
Would he not cast to mole and bat
His royalty, for leave to share
A portion with that beggar there ;
And rags to jewelled robes prefer,
With power to see that rags they were?
The blind are happy, it is said.
Not so this scripture tale has read.
The sharp cry could not silenced be,
" Have mercy, mercy, upon me,
Thou son of David." What he craved
Was met with this, " Thy faith hath saved."

Yet list we to that plaintive cheer ;
'T is wisely spoke and sweet to hear ;
And many witnesses renew
The faith that it is strangely true :
Yes, happy,—cleave we to the hope,
Though feet must swerve and hands must grope ;
All action played behind a screen,
The world no space and life no scene ;
Though nature, art, streets, fields, and books,
And better, best, all friendly looks,
Have faded into nought ; the gaze
That spans a world and threads a maze,
And, when the round of day is done
Outshoots the arrows of the sun,
Changed for the thin short line that slips
Beneath the moving finger-tips.
Who that hath watched the smiles, that chase
Each other o'er the tranquil face
Thus mutilate, does not decree
A place for them in memory?
The human soul a debtor lies
To him who sang of Paradise ;
Who tells you that a single jot
Of heart or hope he bated not.
Nay, there are they whose playful strain

Has argued that this want was gain.
Still Memory's rigid canvas glows,
And Fancy's free conception flows,
And Reason tells her problems o'er,
And gleaning Thoughts find field and store.

What, then? Did our poor Israelite
Prize at too much the wealth of sight?
And is its loss a lighter woe
Than men have thought? Oh no! oh no!
This new Beatitude will prove
The wonder of the Father-love,
That bids such compensation wait
On a calamity so great,
Because so great. Oh! bless the care
That stoops to such a deep despair.
The blind are happy? Only such
As make the world's small remnant much,
And call an inward state to atone
For what makes this without so lone.

Nor all concealed from human thought
How this celestial work is wrought;
They who see not have eyes that lend
Their aid to guide and to defend;
Aye, numberless. They sit immured
In kindly offices; secured
By their strong helplessness. Who stem
The boldest crowds, make way for them.
Mark on the pavement how the click
Of their half-seeing, slender stick,
Is potent as a Sultan's word
Or Marshal's staff or conqueror's sword.
Close tended by the good and kind,
They form the temper that they find.
Does not the disposition bless,
And good-will grow to happiness?
With narrowing range of earth's ado,
The field of strife is narrowed too:
The tents are struck, the flags are furled,
That make a camp of half the world:
As feuds and provocations close,
The unchallenged spirit tastes repose.

The Son of Man, in passing by,
Heeded his suppliant's frantic cry,
Opened his eyes to drink the day,
And showed his following steps the way:
He passes by no more. A sphere
Immortal holds him. But e'en here,
And now, and evermore he stands,
And lifts his voice and lays his hands.
Courage and cure ; But not as when
He moved among those Hebrew men.
No miracle or transient sign
Attest the word or act divine.
The painted earth and painted sky
And looks of dear humanity,
He brings not back ; but shows in light
What needs no orb of sensuous sight.
Ideal growths flush into bloom
And dove-like sits that raven gloom.

O Son of David ! many sit
In that deep valley. Speak to it !
Set Duty's plain and Faith's high hill
Before them ; and within them still
Let Mind pursue its even trains,
Affection chant its sweet refrains,
And Truth draw clear its landscape lines,
Clear as where Nature buds and shines.
From that bright realm reflect a ray
Where tears and films are wiped away.
Let patience hold and love increase ;
And fold them in thy peace, thy peace.

Two series of these modestly called "Metrical Pieces," were printed, the first in 1855, the second in 1870, immediately after his death, which prevented his carrying the volume through the press. The latter contains old hymns in German, which he amused himself by translating as he sat in his chair, blind. They were committed to memory, verse by verse, and then turned into English, the original metre being preserved. Here is a specimen, no better than the rest.

WAS GOTT THUT DAS IST WOHLGETHAN.

(This hymn was written at Jena by Samuel Rodigast in 1675, for a sick friend, who composed the fine melody to which it is set.)

What God doth, it is all well done,
   His will upright abiding :
Since he hath traced my course begun,
   I will go on confiding.
     My God is he
     Who holdeth me :
   I will not turn complainer
   At such a wise Ordainer.

What God doth, it is all well done ;
   He never will deceive me :
In righteous paths he leadeth on,
   And never will he leave me.
     With patience still
     I meet his will :
   Ill days he timely closeth,
   That run as he disposeth.

What God doth, it is all well done ;
   His care will be unfailing :
A Healer, and a wondrous one,
   Will not mistake my ailing.
     No poisons his
     For remedies.
   His truth is my foundation ;
   His grace my whole salvation.

What God doth, it is all well done ;
   He is my light and being.
Mere evil he can mean me none :
   I bow to his decreeing.
     Through weal or woe,
     Time still will show,
   Which every thing revealeth
   How faithfully he dealeth.

What God doth, it is all well done.
  If I must drink the chalice,
The bitter cup which I would shun,
  My shrinking soul he rallies ;
    And, firmly placed,
    My heart shall taste
  That sweet peace in believing
  Which softens down all grieving.

What God doth, it is all well done :
  Strong shall that make and find me.
Rough ways I may be forced to run,
  Griefs pressing close behind me ;
    Yet God will be
    Right fatherly ;
  In death his arm sustaineth :
  Then be it he that reigneth.

I must think that justice has never been done to the purely literary spirit in regard to its influence in preparing the way for the intellectual liberty which we enjoy. Its grace, its sweetness, its love of beauty, its desire for symmetry, harmony, proportion, its hospitality of thought, its refinement of doctrine, its discouragement of the dictatorial temper, are of great importance. In bringing about the Reformation, Erasmus did his part as well as Luther. Luther might expostulate with Erasmus, might laugh at him, might upbraid him as a coward, still it is doubtful if the former could have done his work so well, had not the latter, by his gentle, tolerant disposition, his immense learning, his hatred of excess and partisanship, his habit of applying to all questions the critical method, his respect for reason, his wit and keen satire, leavened and enlarged the mind of Germany. Sweetness and light are no mean powers. The sunbeam daily re-creates a universe, makes the birds sing, the animals rejoice, the forests clothe themselves with verdure, the flowers bloom, and man able to renew his labor. The social world would even come to an end if there were storms only in it, or storms often. Our dependence is on philosophy mainly. It has been heretofore, and it will be so more and more in the time to come. In the second series of his "Essays in Criticism" (The Study of Poetry), Matthew Arnold, quoting himself, thus reaffirming his opinion, says:

The future of poetry is immense, because in poetry, where it is worthy of its high destinies, our race, as time goes on, will find a surer and ever surer stay. There is not a creed which is not shaken, not an accredited dogma which is not shown to be questionable, not a received tradition which does not threaten to dissolve. Our religion has materialized itself in the fact, in the supposed fact; it has attached its emotion to the fact, and now the fact is failing it. But for poetry the idea is everything, the rest is a world of illusion, of divine illusion. Poetry attaches its emotion to the idea; the idea *is* the fact. The strongest part of our religion to-day is its unconscious poetry.

And Mr. F. W. H. Myers, in an article on "Tennyson as Prophet," in the *Nineteenth Century Magazine* (March, 1889), adds his word:

Meanwhile we need our prophets; and the true poet comes nearer to inspiration than any prophet to whom we can hope to listen now. Let his intuitions come to us dissolved in that fineness of thought and melody which makes the highest art we know; let flashes of a strange delight, like sparkles in the stone Aventurine,—reveal at once the beauty and the darkness of the meditations whence the song has sprung. Give us, if so it may be, the exaltation which lifts into a high community; the words which stir the pulse like passion, and wet the eyes like joy, and with the impalpable breath of an inward murmur can make a sudden glory in the deep of the heart.

This is the mission of the great singers, but the minor poets, yes, they who will not call themselves by that fine name, do something to clear the air and render the atmosphere easier to inhale. The lyrical view of religion is the beginning of a new era whose end is not yet, the initiation of a freer movement of mind which detaches intellect from all dogmatism and ensures a perfect freedom.

VI.

THE UNITARIAN LAYMAN.

In 1818 Mr. Frothingham was married to Ann Gorham Brooks, eldest daughter of Peter Chardon Brooks, of Boston. Mr. Brooks was an admirable example of the Unitarian layman of that period, industrious, honest, faithful in all relations of life, charitable, public-spirited, intelligent, sagacious, mingling the prudence of the man of affairs with the faith of the Christian. In meditating on the characters of these men, one is reminded of the good Samuel Sewall. Of course the softening influence of one hundred and fifty years had produced its effect. There was less reference to divine interposition, less literalness in interpreting Scripture, less bluntness, less superstition, if we may use so harsh a word in speaking of that sweet soul. But there was the same integrity, the same conscientiousness, the same directness of dealing, the same respect for learning, the same reverence for piety, the same punctiliousness of demeanor, the same urbanity. They were not reformers, or ascetics, or devotees. All idealists were visionaries, in their esteem. Those who looked for a "kingdom of heaven" were dreamers. They went to church; they had family prayers as a rule, though by no means universally. It was customary to say grace at meat. They wished they were holy enough to adorn the communion; they believed the narratives in the Bible, Old Testament and New. As one recalls the leading persons in Brattle Street, Federal Street, Chauncy Place, King's Chapel, the New North, the New South,—men like Adams, Eliot, Perkins, Bumstead, Lawrence, Sullivan, Jackson, Judge Shaw, Daniel Webster, Jacob Bigelow, T. B. Wales, Dr. Bowditch,—forms of dignity and of worth rise before the mind. Better men there are not. More honorable men, according to the standard of the time, there are not likely to be. Numerous others come up,—William H. Prescott, the Putnams, the Cabots. I used to see people who had the cardinal virtues of the Gospel; Mr. Brooks belonged to this class. It was my privilege, some time ago, to read over his journal and the picture there presented is interesting, not merely as throwing light on an individual character, but also as describing an order of men. There were more distinguished names in literature, in science, in society, but none were more respected for probity, for sterling qualities of character. Edward Everett, one of his sons-in-law, praised him in the *Merchants' Magazine;* Charles F. Adams, another son-in-law, paid him a glorious but deserved tribute.

It is true that the world was small then, and individuals were prominent. But let the world be smaller or larger, the sober qualities of manhood prevail in the long run. If the world be small, the honest man is seen sooner, and comes at earlier recognition. If the world be large, his work and influence are the same. Brilliant gifts produce at the moment a more startling effect, but substantial worth alone endures, giving power and adding to the permanent growth of society. This is not the place to discuss the value of the private person as compared with that of the showy genius, but so much may be said, that unless genius be reinforced by character its impression is evanescent, while character alone furnishes the fundamental basis of development. Confidence is at the bottom of progress, and confidence is won and held by character. It is commonly after a long lapse of time that the contribution made by a high-toned gentleman is acknowledged; then it is, and we wonder that we did not recognize it before. This man's name is written all over the history of his time, when more dazzling persons have passed away. He was simply a merchant, coining money as he had opportunity, buying land, making investments, sending out cargoes, negotiating bonds, pursuing a quiet course, yet he did his full share of public good, and left a name that his descendants are proud to bear.

A few biographical details will make clear their pride of lineage. The ancestor came from England about the year 1630, a sturdy, independent, courageous yeoman. The father was a clergyman, ordained at North Yarmouth in 1764, and settled there five years, when a separation took place, occasioned partly by the condition of his health, which was not good, and partly by his theological opinions, which were too liberal for that region and that age. In 1775 he went over to Lexington on horseback, with his gun on his shoulder and his full-bottomed wig on his head. He was a "Son of Liberty," and stood ready to prove his faith by his works. In 1777 he went as chaplain in the frigate *Hancock*, Captain Manly, was captured by the frigate *Fox*, and sent to Halifax, where, in prison, he had the small-pox. This so weakened his already feeble constitution that he died two or three years after his release, at the age of forty-eight.

His second son came to Boston when about sixteen years old, and boarded with a man who was interested in navigation, an illiterate man, but with business enough to justify his keeping a clerk. From this clerk the boy learned book-keeping. Shortly after coming of age he engaged himself as secretary in the insurance office of Mr. J. H., at the tavern called the "Bunch of Grapes," on the corner of State and Kilby streets. Mr. H. was an old man, and had not been fortunate. At the expiration of a twelvemonth he was advised to give up his business to his energetic, long-sighted clerk. This he did in July, 1789. At this period there was little doing in insurance anywhere, and particularly in Mr. H.'s office, but it soon began to revive under the new management. By and by the French Revolution came, and the war between England and France; commerce increased immensely; premiums went up; so that from 1793 to 1803, the year of the peace of Amiens, the young man, who was now thirty-six years old, with a wife (for he was married in 1792), was busily and profitably employed. To be sure, he had good fortune and excellent friends, but the first was due largely to his sagacity, and the latter to his integrity. He was known to be capable, exact, prompt, and honorable. Mr. Samuel Brown, a bachelor, of great ability and uprightness, much respected and consulted, warmly befriended him, gave him counsel, lent him money. The funding system and the national bank attracted speculation in 1791. Mr. Brown did not personally embark in these schemes, but he advised his young friend to invest, and became his surety for any amount. The issue was successful. Mr. Brooks made money, as he said himself, "hand over hand." In 1803 he quitted the private insurance business, handing it over, in his turn, to his clerk. This was the era of public offices of insurance, a time of peace, too, when ventures were dull.

The interval from 1803 to 1806 was employed in closing up the affairs of the office, and, inasmuch as a good many ventures were still out, this had, in the majority of instances, to be effected by a compromise, the accounts of underwriters being assumed; an admirable plan for the underwriters, who were relieved thereby from all anxiety on account of risks; but, as it happened, an excellent arrangement for him too, as matters turned out well. This, in fact, was the only way of settlement, unless the final closing of accounts should be postponed for an indefinite period until the risks had expired.

The next ten years, in spite of the arduous duties laid upon the President of the New England Insurance Company, were devoted to public service in the Senate, House, and Council-chamber of Massachusetts, in course of which his good sense, business experience, and trained judgment proved of great value. Ability such as his could not fail to be recognized and employed. Money begets money. Success guarantees success. He who can, finds opportunities waiting for him. So his wealth increased, his influence, his honor among men.

This is a remarkable record; remarkable because unusual, for it simply illustrates the old, old truth that industry, judgment, perseverance, integrity, command the world. In 1782 this man came to Boston without a dollar. The country was in the depth of poverty. It was the last year of the war. In January, 1783, a month after Mr. Brooks arrived, peace with England was proclaimed in State Street, but every thing had to be adjusted. This condition of affairs, which must have been an ordinary man's discouragement, was his opportunity. I must quote his own words here:

Having kept books by double entry ever since I had any

money to open them with, it is amusing to mark my progress. I have had the curiosity to note down, not only the progress I have made as to property, but my state of feeling at the end of many of the years. My ledger A I opened January 7, 1788, when I was twenty-one. I had laid up a little by small adventures; my stock was £51, 16s., 10d., about $170. In September 1, 1789, it was increased £380, 12s., 2d., between $1,200 and $1,300. So steady was my good fortune. I believe that every year of my life, from twenty-one, found me richer, and nearly every year much richer. In 1792, November 26th, I was married, and bought a house for £1,000. I think (but have not looked to see) that I was worth then about $25,000, and I felt rich, not so much from having that sum, as from having an income in various ways that gave me perhaps annually as much more. I have indeed been a fortunate man.

True, he inherited an excellent constitution. He very seldom lost a day from ill-health. But, then, he took pains to preserve it by temperance in eating and drinking, regularity of hours, simplicity of living, exercise in the open air, the cultivation of natural tastes, farming, gardening, exhilarating pleasures, sound sleep, and early rising.

He had the best of friends, but he deserved them. They were earned by his fidelity, and kept by his constancy. His exactness, his promptitude, his punctiliousness in detail, his honorableness, his urbanity engaged confidence. He could not give occasion of offence. It is remarkable that he had but one lawsuit, and that was brought by some misguided heirs of an old associate, and in spite of a generous concession on his part. Of course he won the suit, notwithstanding the efforts of distinguished counsel, who could not contest the equity of his arrangements or the clearness of his figures.

> The heirs did not pretend to question the accuracy of my accounts. After searching them with the closest scrutiny, and having every book before them for years, no mistake was found.

A singular feature of this case, and one that shows the innocency of dealing in those old days, was the dismissal by the court of a claim for interest on a large amount for many years. "I had never paid interest to anybody in my life," he says, "and in this case, if Mr. H—— himself had ever intimated such a thing to me, I would not have kept his money a moment. The court decided that I should not be made to pay any." The case lasted four years, and was a chancery suit, where every thing was disclosed. It was gained by sheer force of personal accuracy and straightforwardness of dealing. There was no attempt at prevarication; there was no desire to prevaricate.

There were no wasting sorrows in this life. The father died in 1781; the mother in 1800. She was an excellent manager, with courage to bear the ills of fortune, and with the pride that is a virtue. She taught her children to hold their own, and to be contented. His married estate was happy. His wife had a fund of spirits, was amiable, social, and discharged her various duties for forty years. There were thirteen children, seven of whom survived him; intelligent, accomplished, able, competent men and women. The death of those he lost gave him acute pain, but he was no longer struggling or anxious, and could bring an undiminished fortitude to bear on his grief. Wounds heal soon in a healthy nature.

He joined the church, and was a consistent church member. He was not effusive, demonstrative, or loud-voiced. His name did not stand high on church lists or among the patrons of the faith. His was the calm, rational, sober belief of the thoughtful, educated, honorable men of his day,—men like Lemuel Shaw, Joseph Story, Daniel A. White,—intellectual, noble people, with worthy aims, a lofty sense of duty, a strong conviction of the essential truths of revealed Christianity; sincere believers in the Gospel, of enduring principle, of pure, consistent, blameless life and conduct. Speculative theology he cared little or nothing about. He was no disputant, no doubter, no casuist; of the heights of mysticism of the depths of infidelity, he knew nothing. He was conservative of course, from temperament rather than from inquiry. He took the literal, prose view of Calvinism, and rejected doctrines which did not commend themselves to his common-sense. In a word he was a Unitarian of the old school. Dr. Channing he took no interest in, and less than none in Theodore Parker. Emerson on the one side and Abner Kneeland on the other were about equally far from his sympathies. He was no philosopher. He was no reformer. Political preaching was his aversion; and by political preaching he meant any kind of preaching that dealt with subjects in party dispute. But he went to meeting constantly, and was always in his pew on Thanksgiving and Fast days. He supported the Gospel faithfully in town or in the country; respected ministers; honored the Sabbath. He loved plain, direct sermons, addressed to the heart and conscience. He heard R. W. Emerson, James Walker, F. H. Hedge, William H. Furness, Henry Ware, Jr., but he praised much George Putnam, and E. S. Gannett, liking power that did not run to enthusiasm. But anybody who wore "the cloth" he accepted in silence when he could not applaud. I find this entry made when he was thirty-four years old, and not rich:

> Paid Samuel Elliot, Esq., President of the Trans. Cong. Charitable Society, $50 towards raising a fund for the support of the families of deceased clergymen. I cannot but wish my worthy mother alive, to witness my respect in this small act for that deserving order of men. She had their welfare much at heart.

This may look like more consideration for his mother than for the clergy, but to the end of his life he preserved this old regard, even under what must to him have been difficulties of a pretty serious nature, for he was compelled to hear a good deal of anti-slavery doctrine from his country minister. But he said little about this, or indeed about anything connected with religion. His allusions to that subject were few. His concerns were with this world; and the reality of the other, though regarded by him, must mingle with his daily affairs if it was to be felt. There was no inconsistency, no break, only the one was tangible, the other intangible. His was a strong nature, which absorbed what it could, and took the rest on trust, saying nothing about it. In God, immortality, providence, he had implicit faith, all the more that he was so silent and reserved even in his own mind. He would not commit himself rashly to his private record. On one occasion, when a relative came near losing his life by stepping on the dock too soon from a ferry-boat, he ventured to call the deliverance providential, as if, in ordinary cases, that term ought not to be applied. Supernatural interference with the customary laws that regulated the world was not to be familiarly welcomed. It was there in heaven, but of its action he knew nothing, and had no opinion. If others had convictions, he was glad of it, but such thoughts as he had he preferred to keep to himself.

The feeling of dependence on an Almighty Power, of gratitude to a Beneficent Giver, is repeated every year, as he reviews the past, and presents to his mind a remembrance of good-fortune. The obligation to be just and generous, to consider those who were less favored, to be humble, modest, charitable, is perpetually before him, and always with some allusion to his indebtedness to the Supreme Goodness, accompanied in many instances by expressions of self-accusation. It is evident that the thought of God had much to do with his liberality. The following extracts are interesting on this point:

I have one satisfaction in looking over the year, besides the common one of growing rich, and that is the evidence of having given away a little more than I have sometimes done. In this, however, I have much to learn. One of the best expressions of gratitude to God is to give to the helpless and the needy. However meritorious we may be in the care of our own families and habits, so long as we are wanting in charity to the distressed, our work is but half done. How is it, then, if I know so well what is right, that I no more regard it? I know of no other reply that can be made to this question than this: that those who have been spending a life to get money, and know the difficulty both of getting it and being without it, place too high a value upon it, and cannot bring themselves, at once, to part with it so easily as those who were born with money, and whose knowledge leads to a more reasonable estimate; who view it rather as a means than an end. With rich men it seems to be the object, not to stop when they have enough to afford all the means of enjoyment, but to make every exertion to add more while they fall short of any of their friends. The race, therefore, has no goal. Is this best or not? It is a question not easy to solve. Without a stimulus we are idle, and to be idle is generally to be more or less vicious.

I am worth enough to call forth my sincere expressions of gratitude, and to excite a strong desire to impart to others a portion of my abundance. I regret that I have no greater share of such feelings. That I am wanting in them, I am obliged to confess. Money rarely makes us better.

Evidently this man was not munificent by temperament. The more does such munificence as he had, attest his faith. This is one of the offices of a simple, unadorned religion, to graft on the heart virtues that would not otherwise be exhibited. It is a kind of enforced idealism, imposing qualities the intrinsic beauty of which might not be seen; and thus maintaining a high standard of character quite in advance of spiritual growth. Eventually, far off in the future, the time may arrive when souls will, of their own accord, gravitate towards a large, noble, self-forgetting humanity. But until that day dawns, the ancient law of duty will be in force, and the Commandments will be more potent than the Beatitudes.

It must be confessed that our friend was not one of the open-handed, sunny, exuberant men. He did not belong to the family of the "Cheeribles." As it was, there was more of pity for individual misfortune than of sympathy with general misery, in his composition. All the more credit to him that he remembered the poor, the unfortunate, the sorrowful. It must be borne in mind that he became more generous as he became more rich, which is not the ordinary rule; that he was not rude or sour; that he gave liberally when he thought the public interest would be advanced ; that he gave to institutions of learning and science. His family affections were exceedingly strong. He had no dislike of poor relations; on the contrary, he was glad to help them, and was proud of their good conduct. There are many evidences of his kindnesses to his cousins and nieces, to those who were bound up in the same bundle of life; to those who had served him, or been good to him. A few of these have been selected as illustrating this phase of his disposition, an unusual trait, that is more common in a simple than in a complicated condition of society ; more usual once than now. His attachment to brute beasts is very striking. His compassion for mere poverty was not profuse. Possibly he feared deception. Perhaps he needed to be approached through his personal feelings. At all events, there was no lack of generosity when these were touched, and that these were touched often there is evidence enough. Such entries as these are frequent:

Presented to the family of the late Col. W—, who was an officer in our Revolution, and who left his family poor and two of his daughters deaf and dumb, $100. . . .

For a present, made to a young Doctor P—, who is about to settle at Vassalboro', a most deserving young man but not rich. . . .

Subscribed $2,000. for the relief of the starving poor in Ireland, caused by the failure of their potato crop for two years past. These poor wretches are stated as dying, in great numbers, of hunger. . . .

For a subscription to the sufferers by fire at Fall River, $300. . . .

To Purser Rogers, to aid the friends of the crew of the *Grampus*, sloop-of-war, young Captain Downes, lost at sea, $100. . . .

To a poor man named Wheeler, who saved a young woman, a Miss Graves, a teacher, from drowning at the Locks in Medford, at the hazard of his life, $30. . . .

For $150. which I have done myself the pleasure of giving a kinswoman on her being married. . . .

Mrs. C— G— is dead. This worthy old lady (75) was unable to support herself, being without property and very lame. She had seen better days. For six years past I have contributed $1 a week. Others have done the like or more. . . .

On January 1, 1806, I leased store No. 55 to Mr. J. D., for seven years, at $1,600., a year, having his father as a surety.

Three years, or a little more, have passed within which time J— has failed in business; and having a particular friendship for Mr. D—, who has been made very unhappy by the failure of his son, I have given up the lease and let the store anew for $1,400., making a clear loss to me of about $800. . . .

For this sum, L 1706. 63 s., being what he owes me, and which I have this day made him a present of, and given him a receipt in full for, in consideration of the love I bear him, and of his having been unfortunate. . . .

Paid Dr. J— W—, professor, to aid in his cabinet of minerals, Cambridge, $50. . . .

Mr. B— does himself the pleasure to enclose to Mrs. T— her note for $78, and to ask her acceptance of it. He is happy in giving this small testimony of his respect for her, on various accounts, but especially as being the mother of a young man whose amiable manners and many virtues he shall ever hold in fond remembrance. . . .

We, this day, came into the house formerly owned by Mr. T—B—, who has been so unfortunate as to become a bankrupt. The house was mortgaged to me for its value, and in the sale of the equity of redemption I had no competition. Our going into it therefore is rather a thing of necessity. But it is an excellent house, and we shall be charmed with it, but for the disagreeable circumstance of obliging our friend B— to give it up. We recognize, with gratitude, the happiness we have enjoyed the past summer. No one circumstance seems to have occurred to render it unpleasant. We have both been well with our six children, my business has been pleasant to me, the season has been uncommonly fine, and our friends all about us seem to have shared with us in these great blessings. Seasons of enjoyment so uninterrupted are unusual, and we cannot expect a continuance of them. But should they be afforded us, I hope we shall receive them with grateful hearts, and remember that one of our leading duties and employments under the smiles of Providence is "to do good and to communicate." . . .

The truth is that in putting him into this house my intention was to render the residue of his life a little more comfortable in this regard than it has been for some time past; for he has been obliged, for a long time, to make a remove about every six months. And should I meet with no misfortune, my design is not to charge him with house rent during his life. I hope I shall be able to support so good a resolution. To think that I can, derives to me a most sensible pleasure, for I feel that my present situation has been owing to Mr. H— in a considerable degree, and I should be wanting in common gratitude not to recognize it now that he is old and needy. It affords me pleasure that I have heretofore assisted him, and that I still feel a disposition to do it. It would have been better had I done this before; but I could not find a house, and to make up for it I have, with Mr. Stephen Gorham, paid his house rent for more than twelve months past. . . .

I have concluded to charge no interest, nor any thing, for my services as executor, for a period of nearly six years. This trust has necessarily caused me much care, but it was my determination, from the first, to receive no compensation but the pleasure of serving the worthy family of a friend whom I highly esteemed. This service is among those intended to benefit my friends, and I trust I shall reflect upon it always with the pleasure which generally arises from an attempt to do good. . . .

If my accumulations do not sound so great as in some former years, I have the pleasure to reflect that it is owing, principally, not to my having made less, but to my having given away more. . . .

DEAR SIR :—Inclosed will be my check for $100. which I have the pleasure of offering in aid of the funds of the Congregational Charitable Society. GEO. TICKNOR, Esq., Secretary.

For a donation to Harvard College, $10,000. . . .

For a present made to the Athenæum, with a view to enriching the library, and embellishing that favorite establishment, $1,000. . . .

Contributed towards the Agriculture Hall, Brighton, $100...

BOSTON, July 15, 1818. DEAR SIR:—Inclosed will be found my check on the Boston Bank for $200. My wish is that this sum should be added to the permanent fund of the Massachusetts Charitable Congregational Society. But should it be thought better, by those who have the management of its pecuniary concerns, to dispose of it in any other way, you have my consent. . . .

This sum, $400. I make a present of to my kinsman, from the great regard I have for him, and because he is not rich. . .

MEDFORD, July 20, 1819. DEAR COUSIN:—I have understood from one of your friends, that you are in doubt whether to receive the college prize in a medal or in money, assigning as a reason that you want the money to purchase books. Considering you as richly deserving both the one and the other, I have great pleasure in sending you the enclosed $30, and in congratulating you and your friends, on this honorable testimonial of merit from the first University in our country. . . .

The amount now standing in my books against my brother-in-law, is $20,000. and this is the exact sum he owes me. I have collateral security on his farm, his house, and his distillery, and whenever he pays me the said $20,000. with interest from the first day of April, 1810, I am to give up all these securities. I say "interest from April 1st," because I this day consented to give to him all the back interest, out of affection to him and his wife, and to encourage him in business. He has been unfortunate, but is now doing well. I have no doubt he will be a man of handsome property should his health be spared. And he is so good a man I cannot describe the pleasure I take in obliging him. It is now understood between us that he will pay me the interest on the $20,000. quarterly; and I have, this day, written him a letter, which I consider as binding on me, certifying that the interest is all settled up to the 1st of April, and that the principal is but $20,000. The interest which I have given up to him is about $4,440. . . .

How happy I ought to feel that I have made it in my power

to do an act of kindness to this magnitude ($6,997.50), to an affectionate sister who, I am sure, would, in an exchange of conditions, have done as much, and even more, for me! . . .

For a balance of a kinswoman's account which I have this day made her a present of, agreeably to my letter of this date, which I have requested her to consider as a receipt in full, $557.52. . . .

DEAR COUSIN :—As a small testimonial of my regard, I ask your acceptance of the sum inclosed ; and I propose to myself the pleasure of sending you a like sum once a quarter, for twelve months. Should you, my cousin, be as much gratified in receiving this little present as I am in making it, my purpose will be fully answered. I am, very truly, etc. . . .

These extracts will prove that this man did not live for himself alone, did not live for pleasure or distinction. And if his gifts do not seem large when measured by the criterion of to-day, or by his own means, they were fully as great as the habit of the time warranted. It was a frugal age. There was no interpretation of charity but almsgiving, and that was mainly private. The idea of humanity as a whole, and of the individual's relation to it, was unfamiliar. But the notion that one might grind his neighbors, or make dishonest gain from them, or be indifferent to their condition, was forbidden both by the Old and New Testaments, and though the circle was limited in extent, care was taken that it should not be empty. The present view is broader, but it may be doubted whether conduct more noble complies with the demand for good-will. Fortunes too are much ampler than they used to be, and the sum, though smaller, may be as large in proportion as it is now. The smaller donations were not given out of an abundance, and the number of them was considerable.

For several years Mr. Brooks served the State in the Senate and the House of Representatives. He did not relish political life, and at the close of each session resolved to leave it. His scruples are explained in the extracts that follow.

This day ended the last session of my political year as a Senator. I still say, as I did the last year, that I shall decline another election, if I am thought of, not because I should not be pleased with it if I had the necessary education, but because it prevents the choice of a much more proper man. I confess the office has pleased me, because it has proved the means of some useful knowledge and may be considered as an honor conferred upon me, which never fails to be grateful. But, on the other hand, it is a place which I cannot fill without feeling my inferiority in point of talent, of information, and of influence. After all the peculiar state of parties may induce a request to go again, and my acceptance. I can freely say, however, that I had rather decline. . . .

This day ends the fourth of my political life. It has been passed more pleasantly, on the whole, than any former one. Perhaps every year may render it more and more agreeable. But this, instead of operating as a reason for wishing to be elected again, ought to decide me at once to break off ; for at this moment I am free to confess, however agreeably I have spent my time, that I had much rather stay away than go again. This, however, I may not be able always to say, and by and by I may be left out by my fellow citizens, much to my mortification. I am determined, therefore, to decline standing a candidate another year. I have indeed a hundred reasons, almost, why I should not be a member of the Legislature. I have not the education for it. I have no taste for it. I am not a violent party man. I have numerous calls on my time which do not leave me a moment's leisure, but drive me on faster than comports with my ease and comfort. But more than all this, I feel myself to be in the place of a better man. More than twenty in the town have, in every view, much greater pretensions than I have, and to whom I believe it would be more grateful. . . .

I am brought to the close of another political year, completing five periods as Senator in the General Court. Last year on this occasion I noted down that I should decline another election. Some unexpected incident prevented my adhering to the resolution. I now repeat the declaration that I mean not to be a candidate again. Parties are so equal, however, and the difficulty of changing so great, that I am not certain of having my inclination gratified. When I say it is my wish not to go again, it is not because it gives me no pleasure; for I have been treated with great courtesy, and more respect than, as a politician, I deserve. But I am not fitted for the place. It belongs to others. Others ought to have it. It would please them, perhaps, more than it does me. I have no time to spare, while others have. I want to spend a little time, too, in journeying, which could best be done while the Court is sitting. Another thing is that, in my mind, the honor is not very great. The best men in these times are not in place— certainly not on one side. Men are chosen for politicians who like myself, are too ignorant to undertake anything of the kind. Some of our best men stand aloof. . . .

On Saturday, the 29th of Feb. ended my sixth political year as a Senator from Suffolk, leaving me most thoroughly sick and disgusted with democratic legislation. Where the responsibility is divided among several hundred men, they are found to do things of which an individual would be ashamed.

This day closes my seventh political year, and here I mean to stop. To have taken any part in politics, as a member of the Legislature, was never my expectation, and I think I may add, with truth, it was never my inclination; and, although I have been happy in it as any man could be in times like these, yet various and strong reasons now occur why I should from this time decline. I have been a Senator seven years, which is as long, perhaps, as any man ought to keep in one elective place. I was not educated for a politician, and therefore consider myself, whatever others may think, as filling a place which might be much better occupied by some other man. I may, if I continue, become fond of it, and then should be very desirous of continuing, and mortified if dropped, whereas I can quit now from inclination. This, as regards my personal happiness and the interest of my family, is a most important consideration, and, if I may judge from the effect on others, ought, of itself, to determine me. Last of all, it is a tax on my time, which I think, considering the busy life I have spent, I ought no longer to pay.

The General Court rose yesterday, after a session of nearly fifty days. For the first time in my life I served this year as a Representative from Boston, and I believe I have not been absent from duty a single day of either session. I declined receiving pay, having made up my mind to that at the time of being chosen. On the whole, I have been as much gratified with a seat in the House as I ever was with one in the Council or Senate. They all have afforded me pleasure, though I have not the smallest desire to engage again.

In January, 1821, he was appointed by the Senate of Massachusetts chairman of a committee "to examine generally into the concerns of every lottery now in operation in this Commonwealth." They went to work at once, and reported on February 9th. The chairman enforced the conclusions of the report in a clear, direct, convincing speech, which had a powerful effect. He had been interested himself in lotteries to small amounts. I find half a dozen entries of sums spent in the purchase of lottery tickets. This was a favorite and, it was supposed, an innocent way of raising money for public purposes. It had been resorted to by individuals and by corporations of the highest respectability, and without hesitation, for the furtherance of deserving enterprises, such as the construction of canals, the building of bridges, the erection of college edifices, the repair of beaches. Tickets for lotteries in other States were freely and legally sold in Massachusetts.

It was a species of charity, and was so regarded, not a means of making money without working for the gain. But a keen, practised, business eye saw at once that it was a ruinous way of aiding good causes, and the result of examination was more conclusive on that point than the severest critic could have supposed. There were three great lotteries in the State, the Springfield Bridge Lottery, the Plymouth Beach Lottery, and the Union Canal Lottery. The last, its term having expired, applied for a renewal of its charter; attention was therefore especially fixed on this. It appeared that tickets of all classes had been sold to the amount of $467,328. There had been paid in prizes $406,497. Incidental expenses of management called for $39,988; bad debts were estimated at $24,315; interest on money borrowed to pay prizes, the sum required not having been raised, was charged $2,763. There was consequently a heavy loss to the canal, and the buyers of tickets had, instead of carrying out their intention, been mulcted about half a million of dollars! The other concerns were investigated immediately after, with a result less damaging, indeed, but sufficiently so to discourage enterprises of this kind. This was a fatal blow to the official recognition of lotteries in Massachusetts. It was more than ten years later, however, 1833, before the sale of lottery tickets was forbidden, except of those that were authorized by law. Then the moral question was brought directly up by a fatal issue attending on this sort of gambling. For gambling it had become, a device for growing rich by some turn of luck, as one stands a chance of amassing sums at a gaming-table, risking a little in the hope of drawing in much. For this appears to be the chief difference between gambling and other ventures largely dependent on fortune. Gambling is trust in chance alone, with the smallest admixture of skill, calculation, or sagacity, whereas these rely for success on experience, ability, industry, and foresight. The elements of uncertainty are reduced to the lowest point possible. A perfectly safe business is one that rules them out altogether. Pure speculation must be of the nature of gambling, and all that saves its reputation is the human genius or knowledge or assiduity that in the main accompany its triumphs. These may fail to ensure victory. Luck may go against them; but they are honorable and prevail, whatever may be their present destiny. In 1820, in Massachusetts, lotteries were not looked upon as a form of business, rather as a form of beneficence. There was no rage for them. They did not inflame the popular mind. Their improvidence was more conspicuous than their turpitude. The greater was the merit of warning against them for the welfare of society.

His interest in education, in temperance, in public institutions of beneficence, is abundantly attested by these records. The following entries are curious as illustrating the kind of concern an individual might take in every thing that was conducive to the enlightenment of a community. They embrace all subjects.

On the 28th inst. I was chosen President of the Massachusetts Congregational Charitable Society, instead of Hon. I. Thorndike, deceased. This is a most excellent charity, and less liable to abuse than any one, almost. Its funds amount to nearly $60,000, the income of which is given to the widows and children of deceased Congregationalist clergymen in Massachusetts. The society consists of thirty members, one half clergymen and the other laymen. . . .

Visited Rainsford Island, in steamboat, with Board of Health, Governor, etc. A most delightful day. . . .

Dined at Faneuil Hall. Examinations of the schools. Schools found in a very improving state. . . .

Committee visited State Prison to consider the expediency of enlarging its bounds. Present, Mr. B——, Mr. W——, Mr. T——, Mr. H——; absent, Col. J——. . . .

To Hon. Thos. Cary, to aid a printing press in Cincinnati to oppose slavery, $100. . . .

Our national affairs are bad enough. We have waged a most wicked, a most unjust, a most unnecessary war with Mexico, from which we may not soon come out, and cannot without a vast expense of blood and treasure. By all judicious men this vile contest was uncalled for, and gives the administration great dishonor and disgrace. . . .

Towards curing drunkards, $50. I hope the plan will succeed, but have my doubts.

It appears that this man did what he knew would be for the advantage of his fellow-men, even though he felt no particular interest in it, and had no particular faith in it himself. He was not a sanguine person. But he did not make a phlegmatic disposition an excuse for practical indifference, or a groundwork for contempt of others' efforts, but would lend a hand, if he could not lend a heart. Such a nature is not uncommon, but we do not often see such conduct. Usually, a disposition like his, practical, without impulse, enthusiasm, or imagination, inclined to skepticism in regard to human motives, goes doggedly on its way, pushing claims aside, letting affairs run along in their own way, looking out for the main chance, and satisfied if it can keep on the prosperous side.

He was never satisfied with himself, felt his responsibility, thought he should do more, and threw out his crust of bread with a sort of surly good-will, as if he recognized more duties than he discharged. There is something affecting in such a character, struggling, as it were, against its limitations, with the best of intentions, but with a feeble faith, having the weal of the community in mind, but painfully aware that it could effect nothing except on the plane of unideal achievement, where alone it was strong.

Mr. Brooks was true to himself, sincere, simple, ordering his life according to his own ideas, without regard to the fashions around him.

His dress cost him little. His table was plain, substantial, bountiful. There was always wine with the meats. He rose early in the morning, always went out in summer before breakfast, was scrupulous about his private habits, kept regular hours, and indulged in no injurious excitements. His tastes were frugal, his wishes easily satisfied. One smiles to think how little was sufficient for comfort and happiness in those days, when existence was unambitious and solid. How charmingly innocent all this sounds to-day, when people are so full of pride and emulation!

I may deceive myself, but I think I am worth more than $300,000.; and if so, there is more danger of my having too much than too little. It will not do me nor my family more good, perhaps, if so much, as one-half the sum. I am now thirty-six years old. When I was twenty-one I was not worth one hundred dollars in the world, excepting, perhaps, a small patrimony. How the residue of my life will be spent, after settling my accounts, I cannot at present pretend to decide. Perhaps it would be better for us and our children if I had not half so much. Few can behave with propriety under a change so sudden and considerable. God grant that I may be one of those few! . . .

Took down my boathouse. I concluded, years ago, not to keep a boat any longer. I had no fondness for it myself, nor did I wish my children to have, for fear of accident, and a habit of idleness; and it caused a great deal of care. All these things I ought to have considered before I spent the money. I was in error, and while I acknowledge it fr

I wish I had never committed a greater. The boat, like a thousand other things, disappointed me. I thought it would afford pleasure to us and our friends, but it did neither. . . .

Mr. and Mrs. W—— on a visit of a day and night. Mr. W—— and I rode over to Waltham factory, and through the grounds of Mr. L——. Highly delighted with his grounds, and less delighted with my own.

His affections were natural. He loved his wife, his children, his home, his friends, and took an interest in what concerned them. He was domestic, kind, friendly, in an unostentatious, unaffected manner. This man had deep roots. He was affected by sentimental changes, and showed his emotion by his silence. The following extracts touch the heart :

Perhaps there never was a family who agreed better than ours, or who loved each other more. I never knew the time, for a single moment, that either the mother or the children were estranged from each other, or observed the least coolness : on the contrary, there was always exercised the utmost affection and tenderness. . . .

Had it not been for the untimely loss of our dear, dear little girl, the season would have been a most agreeable one ; but this loss was so extremely painful as to deprive us of all happiness. . . .

Since that time we have been called upon to part with one of our dear children, and that in a way of all others, perhaps, the most afflictive. Our little A. B., aged seventeen months, one of the most lovely babies that we ever had, was scalded on one of her arms on Monday the 8th of June, and continued till Tuesday following, the 16th, when she died, having suffered extremely the whole time. Had this dear child died from ordinary sickness, we should have felt the loss most severely, for she was indeed so pretty and good a child, and withal so healthy, as never to have caused her parents a tear but once ; but to be taken away in the shocking manner she was, was almost insupportable, and what we cannot forget for a long time. . . .

Poor little boy ! while reason would satisfy us, considering the innocence of his life, and our religious hopes, that it is better for him, and we ought not to wish him back, yet passion and feeling, and the recollection of his sufferings, cannot for a long time be overcome or reconcile us to his loss. He was indeed a lovely boy, and it cannot, we hope, be wrong to mourn for him. Does it make any difference that we have many children left? Oh, no ! . . .

In the settlement of my father's estate, the sons had twice as much as the daughters, agreeably to the will. But although in old times the law gave more to sons, and my worthy father might, from law and usage, have deemed it, as doubtless he did, to be perfectly correct, yet at this day I cannot think so, and therefore have now made J— equal to myself.

After this his interest for homely things can be taken for granted. He was fond of agriculture ; he watched the weather ; he rejoiced in the early spring birds, hailing the warmer season with their musical notes.

The robins have eaten up all our cherries. It is discouraging, but we seem to have no remedy short of shooting them, and that we cannot do. The birds give us great pleasure, and we must make up our minds that we cannot have song and cherries too, and there is an end.

He was attracted to the horses that had done him service, and parted from them with pain. To have them killed when useless gave him a pang.

He was not an anti-slavery man ; far from it. He would not have been had he lived later, when the agitation had fairly begun. But he belonged to the party of progress. He was at bottom a Republican, and though he did not believe in the blacks, he believed in an equality of the whites, and desired for all freemen a fair chance. On travelling through Connecticut, he remarks:

> It is, I think, a most valuable and highly cultivated tract of country, and exhibits an equality of condition as respects its inhabitants, which cannot fail to please a man of republican notions.

He subscribed for a teacher of blacks, in 1809, and he treated both races, when dependent, with the same kindness.

To this universal good-will there is absolutely no exception. His courtesy was perfect. In that species of humanity he was really an example. He always returned salutation in form to every one who saluted him. On one occasion, when an old, gossiping, garrulous black man came to see him, on being summoned, he brought a chair, asked his visitor to sit, talked with him pleasantly during his stay, bade him a polite good-by at the front door, then carefully wiped the seat and put it back in its place; thus testifying at once his urbanity toward the human being and his sense of the inferiority of the class to which he belonged. He could not but be courteous, but neither could he forget that there were ranks in society.

In fact, he remembered this faithfully, but in an innocent way, never allowing his respect for rank to overrule his steadfast honor for integrity. Titles without service could not command his reverence. There must be a basis of work. If he loved a lord, paid his court to a governor, admired a dignitary, there was a reason for it, and that reason was manly. When Lord Ashburton came to this country as a special ambassador, Mr. Brooks called at the Tremont House, and was flattered by the friendly recognition, but all the time, it appeared that the nobleman was looked up to as "a blessing to England and the United States, in bringing about a treaty between the two nations." He was convinced that "the Queen could not have sent a better man." A warmer tribute was paid to William Gray, the famous merchant, and to other civilians whose virtues had won his esteem; and if he seemed to set a high value on external dignity, it may have been because of the attention it drew.

It will be divined that asceticism was not in fashion one hundred years ago. Far from it. The old man went to the theatre two or three times to see some favorite actor or popular play. There are two mentions of a dinner without wines. But this kind of abstinence was not common, though temperance was the rule in respectable company. There is a long list of wines in the cellar of the country home, where the most important dinners were given. Though it would hardly match the delicacy of our modern days, yet its abundance will not be disputed.

Every thing like excess in eating and drinking

was regarded with aversion. That it was the custom to give large dinners is evident, and great preparations were made for them. But the amount of gormandizing was by no means in proportion to the bountifulness of the repast.

The dinners of this period, though less elegant and delicate than ours, were as elaborate. Waiters were hired. Cooks were provided. There were several courses: soup, fish, meats, game, pastry, fruits. The household were active in making ready. Hours were spent in feasting, the conversation was brilliant, wit and anecdote flew round much in the English style, though, of course, with a profusion that belongs to a new country rather than an old.

There was a cordial reverence for intellect among our grandfathers. They probably read as much as we do, considering the number of books and the facilities of procuring them. Literature was not copious in those times, neither was it cheap. There was no easy or frequent communication with Europe, or even England, as there is now. Books of travel were very rare, as indeed travellers were. There were histories and poems, volumes of philosophy and sermons, tracts and biographies. If one had no speculative tastes, liked concrete, practical things the choice was narrow; still, cultivation was held in high honor. Brains were uppermost. The libraries that used to be collected, filled with volumes "that no gentleman's shelves should be without,"— Hume, and Smollett, and Johnson, and Shakespeare, and Milton,—though these were little read, was a testimony to the value set upon talent. And when the books, though few, which were selected for their utility or because they expressed individual character, surrounded a man, the tribute to literature was pretty strong. That such were chosen these records show, and those were read. They at least represented something beside ostentation. When a certain fine house was building in New York, a few years ago, the architect took me over it. There was every thing that luxury could suggest in the way of floors, furniture, inlaid woods, marble lintels, draperies, Oriental rugs, carvings, bronzes, mosaics, but there was no provision for the mind. A beautiful library-room stretched along one side of the spacious dwelling, but there were no cases, and no walls for any. In the evening light streamed down from above through stars of glass aflame with electric splendor, but this was for society, not for study. "Where are the shelves?" I asked my companion. "Oh!" he answered, "we have not come to that. It was as much as I could do to persuade Mr. —— to have a library-room. He is a business man." In former days there were books at least. A mute tribute was paid to learning, and in most cases there was something more.

Mr. Brooks attended lectures also, and on subjects far aloof from his daily pursuits. He heard Ralph Waldo Emerson on "The Philosophy of History"; James Walker on "Transcendentalism and Phrenology." He was fond of getting men of intellect about him and listening to their talk. He was intimate with the best minds, invited scholars and statesmen to his table. For works of imagination, poems and the like, he did not care. There was no art in America, either native or foreign, and if there had been it is doubtful if he would have been in sympathy with it, for he was not an æsthetic person. Music had no charms for him. There is no mention of instrument or song. But it is interesting to notice how much remains when these are banished, how much mind there is left, how deep a furrow one can plough without these modern inventions, how much can be done with an old jack-knife, if one has nothing else.

No doubt, according to our definition, he was a Conservative; that is, he was not an Abolitionist, or a woman's-rights advocate, or a radical Republican; he could not answer questions before they were asked. His early years had been passed amid the events of the Revolution and the subsequent attempts to form a government. Then came the war of 1812, with what went before and what followed. And when this was over the original bent of his nature, which was averse to every thing violent or revolutionary, was so confirmed that no excitement could reach him. Yet he was a Unitarian and a Whig, thus belonging to the advanced parties in religion and politics, and went as far as they did sixty years ago. He believed in Dr. Channing and

Daniel Webster, and there stopped with the most stubborn conviction.

"God," said Mr. Emerson "never sends premature ideas." Certainly He did not in this instance. There is no allusion to Garrison or Phillips or Sumner, to the Free-Soil party, or the higher law. If he had been a moral enthusiast he could not have helped showing his predilections. But he was not a moral enthusiast. He was not an intuitive character. He was a friend of law and order. He professed no philosophy but common-sense.

But his conservatism was not based upon position or money or success in the world. It rested upon ideas and upon force of conviction, prejudice it may be, but prejudice founded in judgment. There was limitation, but not assumption; narrowness, but not conceit; rigidity, but not vainglory. He was born in a democracy, and accepted its principles; but if he had been born under king or queen he would have been content with his lot, not feeling himself in bondage, or at all restrained in his activity, though, if his opinion were asked, he would have expressed a preference for republican institutions over monarchical. As a self-made man, he must have believed in the capacity of the people to govern themselves. His faith was in character, not in theory, and as theory comes a good while before character the believer in the last will never be a reformer.

At the end of this long chapter, in which, after all, full justice is not done to Mr. Brooks' charming urbanity, or the delightful Sunday evenings spent at his house by bright people, there is scanty room to tell of the generosity that was displayed by the Unitarian laity in general, both men and women. They all had a genuine desire to render the earthly lot of mankind more tolerable. It is not too much to say that they started every one of our best secular charities. The town of Boston had a poor-house, and nothing more until the Unitarians initiated humane institutions for the helpless, the blind, the insane. The Massachusetts General Hospital, the McLean Asylum, the Perkins Blind Asylum, the Female Orphan Asylum, of which Madame Prescott was president,—an institution that my father was very much devoted to and visited often,—were of their devising. They were exceedingly liberal in their gifts to Harvard College, and to other colleges as well,—for they were not at all sectarian, as their large subscriptions to the Roman Catholic Cathedral proved. Whatever tended to exalt humanity, in their view, was encouraged. They were as noble a set of men and women as ever lived. My single example illustrates them all, in its best traits too.

The married life of Mr. Frothingham was exceedingly happy, the wife's plain common-sense being an admirable complement to his poetical temperament. Her death, which occurred in the summer of 1864, was the first severe blow he was called to sustain. How severe will appear from the following little poem, the beauty of which may excuse its personality.

MADONNA.

The centre of my life, one summer morn,
   Melted from earth into the brightening sky ;
From that time forth its visible round was shorn,
   Narrowing and fading on the wasting eye,
As if no outward scene would care to stay
After that inmost presence passed away.

Oh, daunt me not, ye shadows, as ye fall
   Thicker each day upon my sight and brain,
At thoughts of blank dependence and the pall
   Of utter night, and craze that 's more than pain !
Hide the last ray that guides my footsteps' course,
But spare the wandering thoughts their steadying force.

The fatal loss went first. O shade of her
   Who shone upon my life, its love and saint,
Grow not thou dark to me ! Still minister
   To my lone spirit, burdened down and faint.
Veiled now her very image ; but the heart
Still looks and yearns and moans, and will not part

VII.

THE OLD WORLD.

THE old world was by no means strange to the earlier Unitarian clergy. Mr. Buckminster had travelled there in 1806; Francis Parkman had attended theological lectures at Edinburgh in 1810; Frederic Henry Hedge had studied at Ilfeld and Schulpforte in 1818; Edward Everett had gone abroad in 1815 to qualify himself for his duties as Greek professor at Harvard College. Europe was synonymous with art and beauty and civilization of the aristocratic sort. There were the palaces and cathedrals and galleries and museums. There were the historic cities and fields. There were the great collections of books. There was Athens, and Rome, and Wittenberg, and Worms, and Oxford. There were the Alps and the mountains of the Tyrol, and the plain of Lombardy, and the Italian lakes. But the new world was consecrated to humanity. The American always came back, and was glad to come, not merely because America was his home, and the dwelling-place of his fathers, but because he could breathe freely there. England was still remembered as his enemy; Germany was almost unknown; France was associated with revolution; Italy was dominated by the papacy; Austria was but another name for despotism; the East was a ruin. Then the old world was far off and hard to get at. Travellers across the Atlantic Ocean were few, and the continent was lonely. Railroads were unbuilt and voyaging was slow and difficult. States were cut off from states by vexatious impositions. There was no common coinage, no common law or usage. The soldier was everywhere, the police officer, the priest. Europe was more picturesque than it is now, but far less comfortable. It was different from this country in every respect. The change was complete of language, custom, dress, climate. Here all might be crude, but we had gained in independence, we had won opportunity. The material for every thing good was ours. Whatever man could do was within our grasp. The sentiment of the American is expressed in the following lines written by my father during his first absence.

A SUNSET IN ITALY.

Whence do the Spirits of the Air
  Breathe gentlest, kindliest?
When their wind-harps and balm they bear
  From their chambers in the West.

When glow the many-colored skies
  In their richest beauty drest?
When the sunset flings its gorgeous dyes
  O'er its curtains in the West.

Like that soft air to a weary brow,
    And the throbs of an anxious breast,
Come thoughts of the dear and distant now
    From the home that 's in the West.

Like those fair skies, where to fancy's sight
    Float forms as of spirits blest,
Seems the golden gleam of each dear delight,
    That dwells there in the West.

O land, of all that bright orb gilds
    The freest, happiest, best !
Take me back from the pomp of these blushing fields
    To thy proud shores in the West.

In the summer of 1826, spent with care and afflicted by violent headaches that came weekly, with terrible regularity, Mr. Frothingham sailed for Havre in the packet ship *Louis* for a year of recreation. The voyage lasted thirty days. From Havre to Paris, a distance of one hundred and sixty-two miles, was a journey of thirty hours. Florence was four days from Venice. From Florence to Rome was six days and a half, at the rate of a little more than thirty miles a day. From Lyons to Paris, by way of Moulins and Fontainebleau, was a weary ride of four days and almost as many nights. But this leisurely travelling had its advantages in enabling the tourist to see the country and to stop at pretty places that people now are whirled through. Here is a picture, for instance, of Terracina, the old, dark town on the edge of the Pontine Marshes, which is never seen in our days.

"The next morning we crossed the Pontine Marshes on an excellent road that was thrown across there by Pius VI., and came down in the evening to Terracina. This place is close under the mountains that, a few years ago, were so celebrated as the haunts of banditti. It was three months and a half since I had been in sight of the full sea, and there was the Mediterranean just after a storm throwing up its spray over the very road we travelled. The sun was making a glorious set. The little old city of Terracina, formerly a town, was on the hill behind us, and the boldest height, perfectly inaccessible on this side, was crowned with a very imposing ruin, said to have been the palace of Theodoric the Goth. To complete the picture, a tall palm-tree lifted up its singular branches like an enormous plume above all the rest, seeming to paint itself on the sky."

The travellers were up early, often at dawn of day, and there was a great deal of walking,—fifteen, twenty, in one instance over thirty miles in a day,— with knapsack on back, and over steep mountains. My father always walked when he could, sometimes going in advance of the diligence, thus paying for the privilege of using his feet. All the shorter excursions—to Tivoli, to St. Denis, to St. Germain, were made on foot. He went everywhere. He saw every thing. He ascended Vesuvius. He tramped about Pompeii. He hated Naples, but spent hours in the museum. Rome disappointed him, though he was never tired of St. Peter's.

"November 19th. Yesterday was a great day at the church, the anniversary of its dedication. Of course I attended the ceremony. A great many strangers were there, especially of the English, who swarm here in Rome. Service was performed in one of the side chapels, which are all, of themselves, so many magnificent churches. It consisted chiefly of music. There were two organs, played in concert on opposite sides of the chapel; and two choirs, of fifteen or twenty persons each, sung at the very top of their voices. The show was splendid. Eleven cardinals in full dress were in their places. The papal guards in the Spanish costume, such as it was in the days of the Armada, kept the people in order with their pikes. Ecclesiastical dresses of all descriptions were there to be seen. A cardinal with a retinue of inferior clergy officiated at the altar. But, after all, there was no solemnity in it. The Roman worship is an unintellectual, unaffecting thing when you have made the most of it. All the pomp in the world cannot render it otherwise. The music was as good as the opera, and inspired about the same feelings. The show was not so good as it is there. When a parcel of people are engaged about as many wax lights in bowing and marching to and fro and shaking a censer, and call it worship, it is all one to my feelings whether they are dressed in silver robes or a brown coat. When half a dozen tall men do nothing by the half-hour together but take off a bishop's mitre and put it on again, it does not make the least difference to me that the mitre is blazing with real jewels. . . . Here is a city that has ruled the world twice,—at first by its arms and afterward by its doctrine, and now there is no place on earth that makes one think so humbly of human power, and so contemptuously of human opinion."

If Naples was dirty, and Rome reminded him of the " emptiness of grandeur " and the " transientness of fortune," Paris was a ceaseless entertainment. He went to St. Denis, St. Cloud, Vincennes, Versailles. He ascended all the towers, admired the statues, walked in the gardens. Here is a pretty scene :

"The king had a play in his private theatre on Saturday evening, and I was so much favored as to receive a billet of admission. This was through the kind and unsolicited attention of the American Ambassador, who sent me one of the only two tickets that were placed at his disposal. The theatre was filled from the floor to the ceiling, and with such a shining company as, of course, my republican eyes had never been laid on before. Great numbers of the French nobility were present, and there was a profusion of diamonds and laced coats, you may depend. The entrance of the Royal Family and their coterie was taken notice of in no other way than by the general rising of the assembly, and as soon as all were seated the comedy began. The stage, however, was of small concern to me, whose attention was taken up in examining the actors who did not belong behind the scenes, and especially his Majesty, the Duke and Duchess of Angoulême, and the Duchess of Berri. King Charles is a good-natured, simple-looking man, who laughed heartily at the good things that were said and done, blew his nose with a colored silk handkerchief, and made a snuff-brush of his coat sleeve. The Dauphin is an ordinary personage, who occupied himself chiefly in quizzing the company through an opera-glass. The daughter of Marie Antoinette is a woman of coarse appearance, without the least grace or dignity."

Hence he went to Brussels, Antwerp, Utrecht, Amsterdam, a city not much to his mind. "It began to be built only five or six hundred years ago, on a quagmire that was not worth rescuing from the ocean, and, for aught I see, it is likely, within the same number of years, to be given back to the sea again. Its hackney-coaches are, for the most part, mounted on sleds instead of wheels, that the mud foundations of the town may not be too much shaken. Their sledges are drawn painfully along by a single horse, and the driver, if he may be called so, walks by the side carrying a grease bag for the runners instead of a whip for the horse." He was interested in all the places of historical fame in Holland,—Haarlem, Leyden, The Hague, Delft, Dort,—and from thence sailed to England. There he was as indefatigable as he had been in Switzerland, Italy, France,—wherever he happened to be. He got up early and tramped about in his heavy shoes. He mounted to the top of the Monument in London while the custom-house officers were searching the luggage, and, day after day, went mousing round in search of sights. His activity of mind and heart is unceasing; he goes everywhere, and wherever he goes he makes reflections. Westminster Abbey greatly impresses him, both outside and inside, all but the tombs. "Henry VIIth's chapel is the most exquisite specimen of Gothic architecture that I have seen," he says; but the gloom of the monuments is oppressive to him. Here is a characteristic touch:

"I hate a great parade of sepulchral marbles shut away from the light and air of heaven, under stone arches as proud and cold and dismal as themselves. All this produces in me no emotion but the wish to get out as soon as I can. I connect the show with no ideas that touch me. It is merely gloomy.

> The pillared arches are overhead,
> And under foot are the bones of the dead,

and this is the whole about it. All is stone and stone where all is not dust. For my own part, I love to associate the remains of mortality with the thousand living forms of eternal nature, with the green sod and the fresh flowers, and every thing that springs out of the ground into which man has descended. Let there be monuments, if you will. The more the better. The handsomer the better. But do let the sun shine upon them, and the air breathe upon them. Let me see above them the clouds that are as fleeting as man's life, or the stars that are as immortal as his destiny, and then I can bind together my thoughts properly; then I begin to feel."

Cambridge, Windsor, Eton, Hampton Court, Richmond Hill, were steps in his progress. He walked from Windsor to Stow, from London to Richmond. Then he went to Winchester, Southampton, Netley Abbey, the Isle of Wight, Salisbury, Stonehenge, Bath, Bristol, Chepstow (by steamer at seven in the morning), Tintern Abbey, Oxford, Woodstock, Blenheim, Stratford-on-Avon, where he lingered and mused and wrote the lines to "Shakespeare's Mulberry Tree" (printed in the First Series of the "Metrical Pieces"), Warwick, Coventry, Leicester, Nottingham, Sheffield, Leeds, York, Newcastle. This was the last of England. Then Scotland opened its wonders.

At Edinburgh he did his whole duty: made himself familiar with the old town and the new, visited the tombs of Hume and Burns at Calton burial-ground, went over Holyrood Palace, saw a parade at the Castle, walked up to Arthur's Seat and Salisbury Crags before breakfast, and paid his respects to Sir Walter Scott, who, in answer to his note, wrote a few pleasant lines bidding him welcome as an American and a clergyman; went to Roslin Castle and Hawthornden. From Edinburgh he travelled by mail-coaches to Stirling; walked to Dover (eight miles); took the coach to Callander; walked ten miles, starting at four o'clock in the morning, to the Trosachs, stopping by the way at the spots made famous by Scott's poems—Coilantogle Ford, Loch Vennachar; walked across the mountains to Aberfoyle (five and a half miles); sauntered, the next day, with a pleasant party, through the Trosachs to Loch Katrine; was rowed ten miles up the lake; walked five miles to Inverness, and took the steamer on Loch Lomond to Glasgow, seeing all that was remarkable by the way. After Glasgow, where he was by no means idle, he journeyed through Lanarkshire, Ayrshire, Nithsdale, Carlisle, Penrith, Westmoreland, Preston, to Liverpool. A dull day was passed at Manchester. Then to Chester and Wales. At the vale of Clwyd he took tea with Mrs. Hemans, who wrote him, before sailing, the following pleasant letter:

ST. ASAPH, July 2d,

DEAR SIR:

I regret that it is not in my power to give you all the trouble I had intended; some books which I had proposed entrusting to your care for Mr. Norton not having yet been returned by a friend who had borrowed them. I cannot, however, allow you to cross the Atlantic without bearing with you my best wishes for your prosperous voyage, and my hopes that you may find all the little faces by whose smile you expect to be greeted as bright and blooming as—allow my maternal vanity to say— those of my own boys, with whom you made so speedy an acquaintance. I was not without hopes that you might have returned this way, having very kindly wished you contrary winds and all sorts of contretems to prevent your visiting Dublin, in which case I might have looked for the gratification of again seeing you here; but I am not Norna of the Fitful Head, or you should have had a storm raised to drive you back to St. Asaph.

You will, I am sure, do me the justice to tell my kind friends in New England of the deep and affectionate interest with which I speak and think of them. I believe that a day hardly ever passes in which the names of Mr. and Mrs. Norton are not mentioned with grateful regard at Rhyllon. I should wish my kindest respects also to be offered to Dr. Channing, and to Mr. Bancroft the assurance of our frequent remembrance. Should any friend of yours be likely to visit my own vale of Clwyd, be assured of the pleasure I shall have in showing my regard for your country, by attention such as may be in my power, to his children. And believe me, dear sir, with a gratifying recollection of the hours lately passed in your society,

Sincerely yours,

FELICIA HEMANS.

This letter was received in Boston, whither it was directed. After leaving Mrs. Hemans, the wonders of Wales and the "picturesqueness" of Dublin were surveyed; a few days were passed with friends in Liverpool, and on the 2d of July he was on board the *Manchester*. The homeward passage lasted fifty-two days. The trip was, in every respect, successful. Health had been excellent all the time. A good many agreeable people had been met, some distinguished ones, among them General Lafayette, who called on him in Paris and wrote him two very kindly notes. He had heard the chief singers in the world; had seen the most eminent actors and actresses. He attended theatres and churches in every city, and sought the spots where there was a chance to be amused. He had enjoyed and reflected much, and been enlarged; but the sigh for New England light and liberty was incessant. In one of his letters from Rome he says:

"Of all the cities I have seen I should say that Venice was that for romance, Florence for the arts, Rome for recollections, Geneva for scenery, and Paris for pleasure. But as a place to *live in*, to enjoy one's own self and friends, and bring up one's children, give me my own little Boston before them all."

In the spring of 1849 he went abroad again, this time seriously in search of health. An attack of bronchitis was accompanied with troubles in his head and with indigestion. His strength departed and he was reduced in weight to one hundred and thirty-one pounds. The voyage, by steamer this time, was pleasant. He walked about Liverpool, enjoying the balmy air, and after a ride of nine hours and three quarters, which seemed to him rapid travelling, found himself in London. George Bancroft, successor to Edward Everett, and an old friend, was Minister in England. He saw Mr. Bancroft in court costume,—gold-laced coat, hat, and trousers, with a sword by his side. The next day "his Excellency" took him to the House of Lords. He met Macaulay, Hallam, Milman, and the Duke of Argyle at a breakfast given for him at Mr. Bancroft's.

"Never did I listen to such a torrent of talk. They appeared to talk all together, and yet without confusion. It rushed on from one topic to another with inconceivable rapidity: law matters, church matters, literary matters. I sat next to Milman, who was very kind to me. Hallam opens his mouth and shuts his eyes,—one very large and the other very narrow,—and catches his breath as he talks. But Macaulay! His volubility is charming. His laugh you listen to as a sort of low music. It does not pull you along to listen to it, but you watch it, it is so quiet and pleasant. The engraving that you have of him in the 'History' is a perfect likeness."

He saw and heard Earl Grey in the new and splendid House of Lords. He breakfasted with the poet Rogers, then eighty-five years old, but bright as ever, and "very gracious to me," thanks, it was modestly supposed, to his relationship with Mr. Everett, "whose name is extremely endeared in all quarters." Then he met "his Grace the Bishop of Norfolk, a sprightly old gentleman of seventy," at a breakfast given by Dr. Holland. These "breakfasts" were exceedingly simple, "the utmost extravagance at the rich Mr. Rogers', with a company as numerous as the Knights of the Round Table, was a slice of tongue." On Sunday morning he went to the meeting of the sect founded by Edward Irving, the friend of Carlyle, who died at Glasgow in 1834, and in the afternoon to the Temple, drawn thither by the reputation of the music, said to be the finest in London. The choir sang the tune "All Saints" in an enchanting manner. Westminster Abbey, which had delighted him at first, was thrown completely into the shade. He visited Thomas Carlyle in a most friendly manner and Sir Charles Lyell, heard the opera of "Der Freischütz" sung in the original German by a company from Amsterdam, listened to Lablache the Great, was amused by the dress and style of the servants, and forgot his infirmities for a time.

After sumptuous and finished and blooming England, the first impressions of France, especially of republican Paris, were unfavorable. The swarming people disconcerted him. He saw Rachel at the Théâtre Français and did not like her. But soon his old enthusiasm revived.

"The scene has changed much for the better. I have become used to what was unpleasant, and cannot help admiring this splendid capital. I find vast improvements on all sides: the convenient sidewalks, the well-lighted streets, the omnibuses running in every direction, more commodious and more perfectly arranged than those of London. Then the gardens are finer than ever. The Garden of Plants, the Garden of the Tuileries, and, above all, the Garden of the Luxembourg, branch out with a richness that twenty-three years have done not a little to increase."

He sees Meyerbeer's new piece, "Le Prophète," at the Grand Opera, and its caricature, "L'Âne à Baptiste," meant to pour ridicule, which he enjoyed, on the Socialists and disorganizers of the period. "I suspect that Charles Fourier is held in more honor in

New York and Boston than he is here." The name of Fourier was not musical to his ear. He went to St. Denis, the cathedral of which had been "restored" at an expense, he was told, of more than three millions of dollars. He frequented the Louvre, spent a fête day at Versailles (that demands strength), and saw the sunset from the western terrace of the Palace Garden. "Before me lay the 'Place de la Concorde,' that made my Trafalgar Square appear but a backyard in comparison. The Obelisk of Luxor, brought from Egypt at prodigious expense, stood in the centre. Two grand fountains were throwing up their waters, one on each side of it, the rims of their basins of such a circumference that if one of them was set up in the middle of Boston Common it would appear disproportionately large. Away off at the left were the beautiful porticos of the 'Chamber of Deputies' and the graceful dome of the 'Invalides.' Stretching before me were the 'Champs Elysees.' The marble statues around, much larger than life, received light from the glowing clouds." He took a run down to Tours by way of Orleans. The "Maid of Orleans" was one of his heroines, and he never missed a chance of glorifying the memory of the noble but ill-fated girl and shedding a tear over the spots she had consecrated by her sacrifices. On his return to Paris the city was so disturbed by rumors of insurrection, and by the alarming prevalence of cholera, that he went back to London, travelling on the Continent being rendered uncomfortable, if not dangerous, from troops. In London were friends. He met Mr. Cobden at Mr. Bancroft's, and was greatly pleased with him. He heard Mozart's " Don Giovanni " in German, also Spohr's opera of " Faust." His intimates complimented him on his apparent gain in health. He was delighted with a visit to Milman. " I am much taken with him ; and his house is such a residence as I had never imagined before, a fit residence for a sacred poet, and the historian of two religions. The gate that leads you across the little garden to his study door opens from the very cloisters of Westminster Abbey. His garden walk, with its lines of pointed arches hundreds of years old, is a part of the former refectory of a convent attached to the church. The dwelling itself that he occupies was designed by the founder, Inigo Jones." The Zoölogical Garden was duly inspected and described.

The disagreeable symptoms were all gone. He was weighed, and had gained ten pounds and a half. Still he had misgivings as to his physical condition, and doubted whether he should be able to resume his pastoral duties to any thing like the old extent, and begs his people not to be too sanguine. Before going to the Continent again, he heard Milman preach, and Disraeli speak in the Commons ; melted into tears as the choir in the Temple church sang, "Whither shall I go from thy Spirit"; heard Madame Persiani sing, saw Mrs. Jameson, and had a few minutes' talk with Lady Byron. Then for Ostend. At Bruges he mounted the celebrated belfry, and thought of Longfellow. At Aix Charlemagne came before his vision. But the old town was deserted, dirty, and gloomy. He preferred cheerful things. Belgium charmed him with its picturesqueness and beauty, the elegance of its women, the grace of manners. At Malines there were masterpieces of painting. At Ghent there was a festival with handsome decorations, dances, costumes, banners. At Cologne there was the Cathedral, always interesting and impressive, at that time more imposing for being unfinished and unmodernized. And there was the Rhine, the river he had come to see. This did not disappoint him in any way. He was enthusiastic about the river, as poets are apt to be. He wrote:

"It has not disappointed me in any respect. It has rather gone beyond all my expectations. I enjoyed two days of incessant admiration; from Cologne to Coblentz, where I stopped to rest, and from there to the fine town of Mayence, where I spent another night, I wished I had eyes all round my head, that I might not lose a single point of the prospect. From the seven mountains to 'the castled crag of Drachenfels,' that 'frowned o'er the wide and winding Rhine' (mark these two adjectives), full as hard as I thought it would, to the last gentle slope of the fruitful hills, fruitful wonderfully through the ingenious toil of the cultivator,—every thing was enchanting upon this incomparable stream. I call it incomparable, not because there may not be others as beautiful and noble, though I hardly believe it, but because there is no other the least like it. As the undulating high grounds swept far away, they were thrown up into handsome shapes such as I had never seen before; sometimes rising into the form of a wave just ready to curl and break. You will think me extravagant, but I do really believe that if there was not a single castle or old ruin to be found, and if it was not crowded as it is with the recollections of what has taken place upon its banks and waters, it would still be the most charming of all rivers. One may talk of painting the Rhine,—to be sure the water is clay-color and none of the clearest, —but the thing is not to be done. The *effect* is in no 'Panorama.' And then to think of all the history and poetry that add an inexpressible interest to the whole scene!"

Strasburg delighted him, "French town and yet half German"; the cathedral, which filled him "with special wonder" as a "wilderness of architectural marvels and strange surprises"; the storks; the quaint houses. At Basle he learned of the death of DeWette, who was living but a few weeks before. At Zurich he enjoyed the scenery. At Lucerne he revelled in the view of mountains, lake, villages, chalets, the bridges, the lion,—in the preparation for the more gigantic magnificence of the highest Alps. He ascended the Brünig and the Scheidegg; stood under the deep blue vault of the

Rosenlaui glacier; walked up the valley of Lauterbrunnen; was ravished with the fairy fall of the Staubbach, saw "the incomparable White Lady" at Interlaken; visited the cascade of the Giessbach, climbed up, all alone, to an old ruined castle that was supposed to be celebrated in Byron's "Manfred"; and then went to Berne; saw the bears and admired the spectres of the distant mountains.

"This morning I attended service in the great Cathedral, filled with a Protestant congregation to overflowing. The preacher's old-fashioned ruff was like the past ages; the slamming of the seats as often as the people rose or sat reminded me of what I used to hear in my youth; but the hour-glass at the side of the pulpit looked rather alarming. The minister was merciful, however, and if his sermon was 'as one that speaketh in an unknown tongue,' so was not the organ, a splendid instrument that was installed with ceremony only two days ago, and professes to rival that at Haarlem. The soft tones were like Ariel's and its loud ones made the pews tremble. From the esplanade before the church, or rather by the side of it, one has a superb view of the distant mountains. There is a still better one from a delightful promenade upon the ramparts. To both places I go and keep going. Last evening I was at the latter place from an hour before sunset till no light was left but the moon's, that was too feeble to reflect them well. There they clearly were, with their prodigious masses, and yet hardly looking like real substances. The Jungfrau, the Mönch, the Eiger, the Finster-Aar-Horn, the Schreckhorn, the Wetterhorn, and all the rest of the hard family of the Horns, were right before me, together with the Blümlis-Alp on the extreme right, the most picturesque of them all, as seen from this point. It is an unwearying delight to me to see these tall fellows lifting half of their height into the region of everlasting frost, and with no end of the variety of their appearance, as the sky changes. The clouds try to look like mountains, and the mountains themselves seem sometimes to be but shadows and mists."

From Mayence the voyager went to Wiesbaden in order to see the pleasant place and taste the waters, which were not at all to his liking; nasty tasting things seldom were. At Coblentz he came to "the banks of the blue Moselle" and ascended the beautiful stream, rejoicing to be "water-borne," with "a view all round of heaven and earth"; climbing up to one of the ruined towers before sunrise, delighting in the level meadows, mounting to the Marienburg, and eating his simple meals in the open air, the summer shower moistening his bread sometimes. So he reached Treves,—that ancient city which "Julius Cæsar found important enough to be his useful ally,—a city where false Constantine displayed his imperial state and cruelty, and where some of his successors resided; a city whose archbishops were princes and fighters, men of stratagem and violence. Have I not been into its Cathedral and its Church of the Madonna over and again, and heard the music and singing therein? You need not desire to look at two more impressive specimens of ecclesiastical antiquity, built in the depths of the dark ages. But they are quite young when compared with the Roman remains that stand yet in the town. I have been to the amphitheatre, where beasts and men tried which could be the most savage, fifteen hundred years ago the scene of vast bloodshed and mortal agony. I have been to the mighty skeleton of the Baths, built as none but those gigantic robbers knew how to build. I have been to the top of the enormous gateway of which no tradition gives the slightest account. . . . Before leaving Treves I may as well mention that here was the ridiculous exposition of the 'Holy Coat' that made so much commotion a few years ago, and that exalted one Mr. Ronge into the fame of a second Luther for several weeks."

The hours in Metz were not many, and they were very much occupied. The traveller was glad to find himself in cheerful France again. Paris was an old story; but "Chalons upon the Marne" was not; Rheims was not. Did not Joan of Arc have her great day there? Was not the grand cathedral there? and the statues? and the painted glass? and the fine round window?

In the summer of 1849—August 22d—the Peace Congress met in Paris, and the Rue de la Chaussée d'Antin, where the meetings were held, was alive with people, among whom, as much interested as anybody in the humane aspect of the reform, stood Mr. Frothingham, not a representative but a spectator only. Victor Hugo, in a white vest, light trousers, with dashing stripe at the side, presided and opened the proceedings with a characteristic speech. He was supported on the right by the Roman Catholic minister of the Madeleine, in priest's dress, with a large black band edged with white, and on the left by Athanase Coquerel, the Protestant preacher of the Oratoire, wearing in his button-hole the badge of his membership in the National Assembly. The utmost harmony prevailed throughout. The speaking was partly in French and partly in English, and as the orators did not always understand each other, there could be no collision. Strictly speaking there was no debate, for discussion of the existing state of politics was forbidden, even if all controversy had not been ridiculously out of place in a peace convention. The English spoke wonderfully well. The French language lent itself easily to noble declamation. The Americans were voluble and sentimental. Henry Vincent distinguished himself. There was great applause and unbounded enthusiasm. Every enunciation of a generous principle was greeted with rapture. Even platitudes were welcomed. All the idealists and inflammables were there, or wished they were. Hundreds had crossed the Channel; one of the French newspapers hailed the Americans who had bravely come from the " depths of their forests."

The French ministers showed all honor to the visitors. The public works were, without reserve, thrown open on presentation of the little blue ticket that the members carried. The "great waters" at Versailles celebrated their coming, and a breakfast was given them. The palace of St. Cloud flung wide its gorgeous apartments, glowing with paintings and glittering with gilding. The crowd stood on balconies which looked over a charming country as far as Paris. The procession marched through the lovely grounds, and round the lake, encircled with statues and fountains. From a deep grove, approached by a noble flight of steps, a solitary jet of water, the highest in France, tossed up its spray for the delight of the spectators. The cascades were illuminated. The waters fell down three long flights of steps. Lights were placed in a row on each stair, so that the waves rolled over them, while innumerable fires shed their lustre upon the surface. At intervals masses of flame, variously colored, went up from large vases above and below the fall, lighting up not only the streams and the vast basin they flowed into, but the trees that made an amphitheatre at the side and behind. The whole was like a scene of enchantment,—a rare sight for the French themselves; a little showy perhaps, but very splendid.

This was the glorious side. The droll aspects of the Congress may be forgiven,—the strange mingling of tongues; the mistake of Mr. Cobden in announcing a letter from the Archbishop of Paris as a communication from the Archbishop of Canterbury; the heated harangue of a socialist; a denunciation of American slavery by an Abolitionist; the accidental assumption of borrowed plumage by a few unpacific individuals. But an incident that befell my honest, guileless, simple-minded father was so characteristic and so funny that it must be told. M. De Tocqueville, Minister of Foreign Affairs, had thrown open his magnificent rooms and illuminated his garden, and given a most hospitable invitation to the "Congress." An officious person, who seemed to be a master of ceremonies, advanced, called the visitor by his name and title, and presented him formally to the host and hostess. This person proved to be the editor of an anti-slavery sheet, and not a very savoury individual either. Both these facts were learned afterwards to the victim's great disgust. It is not likely that M. De Tocqueville knew who his usher was, being absorbed in the agreeable duty of receiving the men and women who represented a great idea.

This description of Victor Cousin is interesting. Cousin, it may be necessary to remind the present generation, was a famous philosopher, a correspondent of Dr. Channing, a man of influence among the early Unitarians, one whose works were studied by scholars, fifty years ago.

"He lives at the Sorbonne, an ancient sort of college, where I found him after mounting but one flight of homely stone stairs. His reception-room was as plain as plain could be, with a few common engravings, likenesses of uncommon men in his line, hanging on the walls. The only two engravings of a different sort that he had chosen to deck his room with were the 'Death of Socrates' and the 'Madonna of the Throne.' He received me with great cordiality, in a queer cap covering his gray hair, and wrapped in a gown not unlike the poorest that I have sometimes ventured timidly to make my appearance in on a winter morning. He talked with great animation on religious philosophy in general and on some of my Boston friends in particular; putting on no dignity or reserve, but throwing himself about with a liberality of gesture and grimace that would have seemed rather odd in England or America. I was very much pleased with what he said, and believe that I was rather lucky in the small part that fell to myself in the conversation."

He went to the Théâtre Français to see Mademoiselle Rachel, who had reappeared in Corneille's tragedy "Les Horaces," and liked her better than before, but was not transported. She was too distressing for him, nor did her spasmodic power please his taste, which demanded more even as well as more cheerful things. Here is a picture of Napoleon III:

"Whoever has seen any of his pictures has seen *him*, with his ordinary features, and narrow, heavy eyes;—a sluggish-looking countenance. He is any thing but sluggish, however, in reality. He affects state, never forgets the name of his uncle, who is the national idol, and doubtless has the most ambitious views. One of the French papers that I read this morning contrasted his military trappings and attendance as he parades through the country whenever a new section of railway is to be opened, with plain General Taylor, the old soldier and conqueror, visiting different parts of our United States without pomp or noise."

A night or two more at the Grand Opera, the Gymnase Dramatique, where the acting was perfect, excursions to Fontainebleau, St. Germain, Passy, Neuilly, Chartres, Rouen, and the traveller bade farewell to France and looked toward home. The last letter was written. England did not detain him long. He sailed from Liverpool in September. The trip was, on the whole, beneficial, though it did not restore him. In the latter part of the summer, he spoke of feeling well, but of being far from strong; doubted if his voice was more powerful than it had been before he left Boston; and was afraid lest his people should think him more vigorous than he was; talked of a colleague, and of holding out for a year alone. The Atlantic voyage was prosperous, but a slight shock at the end showed how weak his nerves were. He was in no condition to resume parish work. Candidates for the pulpit preached for two or three years, and in May, 1853, Rev. Rufus Ellis was installed as sole minister of the First Church. The meeting-house in Chauncy Place was torn down in 1868, and a new dispensation of Unitarianism ensued, more "evangelical" than Dr. Frothingham's, while the new edifice on Berkeley Street called for a less simple ceremonial than had prevailed in Puritan times.

The next years were uneventful. The parish work was done by another; but there was opportunity for friendly service among the parishioners, and for kindly counsel and help toward his new successor. Then he could read his books and cultivate his friends.

In 1859 a third tour of eighteen months in Europe was made with his wife and daughters. Some new places were visited as a tourist might do, but nothing of moment occurred to be recorded. In Rome he was attentive to Theodore Parker, who was that winter trying desperately to recover his health in the "Eternal City." It was in the course of this journey that Dr. Frothingham became first aware of a defect in his own vision. He could not enjoy picture-galleries, saw figures distorted and colors blurred; but his sweetness of disposition turned this off, and even made fun of it. Still he felt uneasy, and finding that the disability was due to no local or incidental cause, consulted the best oculists in Paris and London, but without success, as no disease was visible in the organ itself. The malady afterwards proved to be more deeply seated, but when he came home in the autumn of 1860, the dimness, though increased, was not alarming. The event was not anticipated by anybody, and the malady itself was quite forgotten in the joy of getting home; for home meant peace and friendship and quiet studies and tranquil thoughts and loving duties and sweet cares. There was, in all his wanderings, the last as well as the first, a longing for these, that is expressed in the following little poem, one of several written in the Old World, and expressing his deep affection for the New, an affection which all his companions felt, for they were devoted friends of republican institutions, staunch defenders of intellectual liberty, all ardent advocates of intellectual liberty, and serious champions of social and domestic virtue. The great words, "home," "peace," "order," "union," "love," "enlightenment," were dear to them. They abhorred violence, discord, disruption, and, if they were conservatives, were conservative of what seemed to them altogether good; and although to ardent reformers it did not appear to be the best by any means, yet there is something touching in the patient allegiance of these men to the primeval virtues. They adhered to certain cardinal sentiments, dreading innovation because it involved uncertainty. They were not valiant men. On the contrary, they were timid and apprehensive, fearful of change. They did not see far or search deeply. They took for granted many things in religion and in society that are disputed now. They were not more comfort-loving than others, but they kept behind the intrenchments, and did not venture beyond the lines. Agnosticism was unheard of, nor could they conceive of a religious man who was a doubter of the Christian authority or the leading tenets of theism. Naturalism was a thing abhorred, and the least approach to Socialism was detested. They snuggled in the nest of faith. This nest was composed of the refuse of larger growths—of twigs, straws, leaves, an occasional flower, a bit of sprig; but they were happy in it, for the permanent part consisted of home feelings, of sympathy, affection, sweetness, peace, hopefulness, placid contentment, submission to a divine will, cheerful anticipation of immortality.

HOMEWARD FROM FOREIGN LANDS.

"Then I said, I shall die in my nest."—JOB xxix., 18.

There are they who have left their sweet home,
Through these strange, distant places to roam,
And no more back, no more, ever come ;
And I sigh with their memory oppressed,
    "Let me die in my nest."

When the troubles of nature are rife,
And the heart with itself is at strife,
For then Death is in conflict with Life,
I submit to the sovereign behest,
    But would die in my nest.

Where within me the first thoughts were dreamed,
And upon me Affection first beamed,
And through blossoms and tears my spring teemed ;
Amid scenes and companions loved best,
    I would die in my nest.

Not in lands with a speech not my own,
Where the sights that are newest look lone ;
But where all most familiar had grown
To my eyes and the throbs of my breast,—
    Shall I die in that nest ?

They will say : " It is one to the wise
From what country the freed spirit flies,
For the way is the same to the skies " ;
Truths to faith and to reason addressed,—
    But alas ! for the nest.

Oh, methinks it would glad the last gaze,
To be circled with friends of old days,
And the spots that are gilt with the rays
That stream from the sun of the West
    O'er the down of my nest !

And I hear a propitious decree ;
And the blessing I hoped for shall be ;
For I smell the wide air of the sea.
There is land o'er the waves' foamy crest :
    " I shall die in my nest."

Thus far Dr. Frothingham's lot had been a happy one. He belonged to an honored profession; he was most respected; he was cordially beloved, as a charming person; his temperament was sunny; his home was peaceful and affectionate. He lived in a delightful street, well called "Summer"—a street of gardens, and elm trees that branched over so as almost to meet across the way; with Edward Everett next door, and excellent people on either side. An air of Oriental magnificence was imparted by Mr. Cushing's Chinese servants in their native dress.

VIII.

THE FREEDOM OF FRIENDSHIP.

The literary quality of this form of Unitarianism is nowhere better seen than in the spirit of natural friendliness that took the place of sectarian combination. Of course this was confined to the cultivated men, for with humanity at large there was no active sympathy. There was pity but little fellowship. Here, too, I must take my father as a representative; who, though he was more poetical than his companions, illustrated their breadth of interest. With Henry W. Longfellow there was always an affectionate intimacy; partly due to the professor's position in the neighboring college of Harvard; partly to the poet's genius; but more to the warm, exuberant temper of the man and his enthusiastic interest in all humane learning. He was delighted to meet Cornelius C. Felton, "heartiest of Greek professors," as Dickens called him,

> So wholly Greek wast thou in thy serene
> And childlike joy of life, O Philhellene!

to quote Longfellow's sonnet to him. W. H. Prescott was a loved form. Ticknor was admired for his knowledge of letters, and Hillard for his elegant scholarship, and Everett for his fine taste and his eloquence, and Palfrey for his erudition, and Bancroft for his brilliancy. The clerical intimacy was large. In an unpublished poem, written some fifty years ago, there is a sketch of "nine worthies,"—S. K. Lothrop, Chandler Robbins, Ezra S. Gannett, Ephraim Peabody, Cyrus A. Bartol, George Putnam, William P. Lunt, James Walker, Alexander Young. In an old album of portraits I find photographic likenesses of Dr. Kirkland, Dr. Pierce, Dr. Freeman, Dr. Porter, Dr. Harris, Dr. Gray, Dr. Channing, Dr. Lowell, Dr. Parkman, Dr. Ware, Dr. Greenwood, James Walker, John Pierpont, S. K. Lothrop, Chandler Robbins, E. S. Gannett, Cyrus A. Bartol, E. Peabody, Samuel Barrett, Wm. P. Lunt, George E. Ellis, Alexander Young, Convers Francis, Jared Sparks, R. W. Emerson, George Ripley, F. H. Hedge, Orville Dewey, Rufus Ellis, Edward E. Hale, T. S. King, Theodore Parker, F. D. Huntington—a rich brotherhood, and miscellaneous; but the unsectarian heart embraced them all, having regard more to the purpose than the creed, though this too, within Christianity, was imperative. Of those with whom my father was more or less intimate, some are the subjects of written memoirs, some are illustrious, some are comparatively unknown. All had high ideal aims. Everett was originally a clergyman; so was Palfrey; so was Sparks. Geo. Bancroft thought of the ministry at one time, and preached several sermons. The names of Samuel Barrett and Caleb Stetson are almost forgotten now; but once they were important and even conspicuous men. His friend, Lewis G. Pray, wrote a memoir of the first, editing, along with it, ten of his excellent sermons; and the other—a witty, genial, humane man, did good service as an opponent of slavery, and a transcendentalist.

There are still traditions of the wit of FRANCIS PARKMAN, but how few know that he was one of the eminent characters of his time! He studied theology under the direction of W. E. Channing, entered his name in the school of divinity at Edinburgh, and, in the course of the session there, read a discourse that received the approbation of the professor. In 1812 he preached several Sundays for the Unitarian society in Liverpool, of which Mr. Lewis was pastor, and with such acceptance that he was invited to remain as associate minister. Declining this call he came home, preached for a considerable period at the First Church in Boston, then vacant by the death of William Emerson. Soon after, he was ordained and installed as pastor of the New North Church, in Hanover Street, as successor to Dr. Eliot. Mr. Channing, his old instructor, preached the sermon of ordination. Mr. Parkman (he was made a D.D. by Harvard College in 1834) was a man of various information, a kind spirit, singular benevolence, polished yet simple manners, fine literary taste. He was a small figure, with a pleasant voice, a gracious manner, and an expressive face. He was subject to moods of depression, as men of mercurial and humorous disposition are apt to be. Rev. F. D. Huntington (now Bishop of Central New York) wrote this of him in 1854 to Rev. Dr. Sprague, author of "Annals of the American Pulpit." Mr. Huntington was then a Unitarian minister.

> His pleasant familiarity never transgressed the bounds of perfect courtesy ; and, even in the less restrained hours of intimate fellowship, something was always present in his deportment to betoken his excellent professional breeding. It was his custom, indeed, to insist with considerable scrupulousness, on those clerical proprieties and formalities that formerly, more than now, distinguished the ministerial vocation ; and those whose taste in other respects was less exacting than his own, will long remember the good-natured rebukes with which he pursued their departures from the ancient rule.
>
> . . . .
>
> He loved Scriptural quotations in all conjunctures, and was sometimes tempted to use them rather by their appositeness, than by the solemnity of the circumstances. He kept the attention of the company always awake by piquant terms of expression and quaint phrases, nor was his wit or eloquence wanting when the tone of the talk was raised. He had an admirable faculty of describing the peculiarities of public men, and the former events with which he had been conversant. Of personal anecdotes he held at command a large fund. These remarkable conversational gifts, together with his gentle social connections, contributed to the eminence of his position, both in England, where he was much respected, and among literary associations at home. As a preacher, Dr. Parkman was uniformly serious and practical. In his long ministry at the "New North," his fidelity and devotion were untiring, as both the living and the dead would affirm. There was great method in his habits. He was a genuine respecter

of humble virtue. He honored the poor saints. He blessed the widow and the fatherless. He was prompt in all the affairs of consolation and charity. Family wealth never weakened his work, nor enticed him to forget the claims of the least conspicuous of his flock, and that is no light honour to his Christian conscience ; but it did make him the constant and munificent guardian of penury and distress.

. . . .

Every aspect of suffering touched him tenderly. There was no hard spot in his breast. His house was the centre of countless mercies to the various forms of want ; and there were few solicitors of alms, local or itinerant, and whether for private necessity or public benefactions, that his door did not welcome and send away satisfied.

. . . .

In the Trinitarian controversy he did his share on the Unitarian side. For nearly half a century he contributed more or less to the principal religious and theological publications of his denomination. The processes of his mind were practical, however, rather than speculative. His style was not wanting in force, but distinguished rather for clearness and ease.

Many of his papers were biographical, narrative, or commemorative. He looked at the varied questions of Theology, and at ideas and principles, very much in their relation to persons. He spoke extemporaneously with great readiness and often.

. . . .

Harvard University, of which he was an Overseer and frequent visitor, was very dear to his heart, and its concerns touched his personal pride. Throughout he was a zealous and consistent friend of the Unitarian movement ; but was too catholic in his feelings to favour an exclusive policy towards any Christian sect.

. . . .

Those who ever joined in Dr. Parkman's public prayers, would feel any notice of him to be incomplete that did not advert to the beautiful and affecting union of fervour and simplicity, biblical phraseology and varied allusions with ever appropriate reference to circumstances and persons, which marked his petitions and thanksgivings. I remember that the Rev. Dr. Henry Ware, Jr., professor at Cambridge, on the Parkman foundation, procured from him a letter giving his conceptions of that exercise, and his own mode of preparation, and that this letter was read by Dr. Ware to the successive classes of students in the Theological School.

Edwin P. Whipple, an excellent critic and a candid judge, expressed himself as follows :

His prime quality was humour ; and humour, not merely as a power of his mind, but as an element of his character, and an instinct of his nature. In him it seemed made up of feeling and insight in equal proportions. In its most intellectual manifestations it evinced that its source was in a kindly, tolerant, and beneficent disposition; that it loved while it laughed. Whether he conversed on theology or politics, or manners, or individual character, or recorded some sad or pleasant experience of his own, the wise and genial humorist was always observable, softening, enlivening, enriching every thing he touched. His practical discernment was so sure and keen, his knowledge of the world was so extensive, and his perceptions of character and motives were so quick and deep, that it was impossible to impose on him by any pretence or deception. With all his subtilty, however, in detecting the weaknesses of men, there was nothing of the satirist in his disposition ; and those who were the objects of his shrewd but kindly humour seemed to enjoy it as much as others. He so softly let a man down from the stilts of his rhetoric, or pierced the bubbles of his declamation with such smiling tact, that the person felt the mists of his self-delusion scattered as by sunlight. It was impossible to meet Dr. Parkman in the street, and stop a minute to exchange words with him, without carrying away with you some phrase or turn of thought, so exquisite in its mingled sagacity and humour that it touched the inmost sense of the ludicrous and made the heart smile as well as the lips. Indeed, in this respect, he continually reminded me of some of the greatest and most genial humorists in literature,— of Addison and Goldsmith, of Lamb and Irving. In the commonest conversation, his mastery of the felicities of humorous expression was quite a marvel. Without the slightest hesitation, sentence after sentence would glide from his tongue, indicating the most consummate command of the resources of language, and every word moistened with the richest humour, and edged with the most refined wit. His voice, in its sweet, mild, unctuous smoothness, aided the effect of his expression. His style in conversation, unlike his style in his writings, evinced a creative mind. It was individual, original, teeming with felicities of verbal combination, and flexible to the most delicate variations of his thought. Though it owed no small portion of its charm to his inimitable manner, it still, if literally reported, would have possessed sufficient vitality and richness to indicate, better than any printed memorials of his powers, his real wealth of thought, observation, experience, and knowledge.

James T. Fields used to delight in repeating a charming illustration of Dr. Parkman's mingled gravity and humor. He said that when he first came into service as a young store clerk in the Corner Book Store, Dr. Parkman, who was a stranger to him entered, and addressed him thus:

"I am in want, as a gift for a maiden who is about to be married, of a copy of a book once held in high regard, but now, I grieve to say, much neglected and forgotten—the Holy Bible, an Oxford edition, well clothed in its binding, appointed to be read in churches. Have you one?" The youth looked at him in awe, and climbing a ladder, took down a copy from a top shelf. Being not then familiar with the private trade-mark giving the price of the book, he scanned the mark on the inner cover, and raised his eyes musingly to interpret it. Dr. Parkman, as if protestingly, said : " My young friend, you need not invoke divine aid in fixing a high price on that volume. It seems to me a little shop-worn."

Here is another good story. Dr. Parkman was walking with a fat brother; the day was warm; the companion panted, wiped his face with his handkerchief, and manifested other signs of suffering. Dr. Parkman said to him:

"My friend, it has pleased Divine Providence to endow you with an ample fleshly integument. How happy you must be to remember the apostolic promise that *we shall be changed!*"

ALEXANDER YOUNG used to be a prominent personality in this Zion. I can see him now, with his rather short but broad, thick, stocky, and seemingly robust frame, his portly shape and somewhat heavy features, walking, with stately tread, down Summer Street, where he lived and where his meeting-house stood. He was a scholar, and not in New England history alone. I remember his expressing an opinion about a nice point in French pronunciation at our house one day. He lived but fifty-four years, and did an immense amount of work. He was the son of a printer, was educated at the Boston Latin School, left Harvard College in 1820, the companion of E. S. Gannett, W. H. Furness, E. B. Hall, leaders of the Unitarian faith, studied divinity, was approved by the Boston Association, and from the start was so popular as a preacher that in two months after entering the profession he received two invitations, one from the Twelfth Congregational Society, the other from the New South. The last he accepted, and became the successor of Kirkland, Thatcher, and Greenwood. Here he preached nearly thirty years—from 1825 till 1854, and was so little polemical or doctrinal that he did not care to make any public statement in regard to the details of belief. His main interest, outside of his profession, was history. The series of "Selections from the Old English Prose Writers," in nine volumes, published in 1839, not only showed great powers of discernment and a delicate appreciation, but helped to educate people up to such masterpieces as Sir Thomas Browne's "Urn Burial," Sir Philip Sidney's "Defence of Poesie," Fuller's "Holy State." His "Chronicles of the Pilgrim Fathers of the Colony of Plymouth from 1602 to 1625"—published in 1841 (a second edition appeared in 1844)—elicited warm commendation from so exalted a judge as Hon. R. C. Winthrop. In 1846 was published "Chronicles of the First Planters of the Colony of Massachusetts Bay, from 1623 to 1626." Materials for two other works were collected, and the works themselves planned: "Chronicles of the First Planters of the Colony of Virginia, from the First Voyage of Discovery in 1584 to the Dissolution of the Virginia Company in 1624"; and "Chronicles of Maritime Discovery on the Coasts of

North America," but untimely death prevented the execution of either of these tasks. The volumes published showed extensive and accurate knowledge, extraordinary zeal in research, singular impartiality of judgment, great activity of mind in the direction of literary achievement, a strong inclination towards ethical as distinguished from speculative subjects, a passionate love of books and elegant letters. A contemporary remembers him as a "highly gifted and accomplished man," and praises his "gentlemanly manners" and the "genial and kindly tone of his spirit." Dr. Young—he was made a Doctor of Divinity in 1846 by Harvard College—was decidedly Unitarian, of a conservative stamp, but was never sufficiently interested in dogmatic questions to take a prominent part in controversy. Such agitation was not conducive to his favorite pursuits, to say nothing of a constitutional dislike to extreme opinions. One does not hear of him in connection with new schemes of philosophy or movements for social reform. His faith was in slow methods of influence, in education, cultivation, the spread of intelligence, the increase of self-respect. With the whole weight of his moral sentiments he repudiated Calvinism, thus exalting the natural mind above ecclesiastical authority as it existed in his time, without pushing the lines of logical inference further towards their conclusion, as Parker, for example, did. With neither Channing nor Emerson was he in sympathy; but he used faithfully every gospel appliance for elevating and reforming mankind. His attitude toward Scriptural authority is explicity declared in a sermon preached at the ordination of Rev. George Edward Ellis, as pastor of the Harvard Church, in Charlestown, March 11, 1840:

> The Christian minister is to preach the declarations and statements, the doctrines and principles of the Gospel. In his view, religion is identified with Christianity, and he values Christianity because it gives him assurance of certain truths which he regards as of infinite importance. These truths constitute his religion. . . . All our knowledge of Christ and Christianity is derived, not from consciousness or intuition, but from outward revelation. It is not innate, spontaneous, and original with us, but extrinsic, derived, superinduced. . . . Once admit that the New Testament does not contain all the principles of spiritual truth . . . and you open the door to all sorts of loose and crude speculations. . . . The old heathen sages, it is true, stumbled on some fortunate conjectures, and made some happy guesses, but they could assert nothing with assurance; they could not speak with *certainty* and *authority*.

This is the very ground taken in Mr. Norton's "The Latest form of Infidelity," 1839. Mr. Ellis' sermon on Dr. Young, preached at "Church Green" on March 26, 1854, the Sunday after the interment, reiterated the same ideas:

> With an intense and unwavering conviction he held to the divine mission of Jesus Christ, confirmed by miracles, illustrated by inspired teachings, and made essential to us by our spiritual needs and by the imperfection and insufficiency of all earthly dependence.

At Dr. Young's death there was a general expression of bereavement. Funeral discourses were delivered, tributes were paid, notices were written, the newspapers spoke in his praise, and he who had shown such excellent judgment in celebrating distinguished men was himself distinguished. Dr. William B. Sprague gave him a place among the eminent Unitarian divines in his "Annals of the American Pulpit"; Hon. Robert C. Winthrop, who had known him well for several years, wrote of his "sterling qualities," and said:

> No man among us had a more familiar acquaintance with the treasures of English literature. The series of selections from the Old Prose Writers, which he published in 1839, gave ample proof of his careful discrimination and refined taste, while it introduced to the reading community of our country some of the choicest productions of the English language. I have a vivid remembrance of my own sense of personal indebtedness to him, as I read, for the first time, in this edition, such works as Feltham's "Resolves," and Fuller's "Holy State," and Sir Philip Sidney's "Defence of Poesie," and Sir Thomas Browne's "Urn Burial."

Mr. James Russell Lowell took pleasure in confessing that he owed much to the same collection.

Dr. Young took an active interest in every thing that concerned the highest education. He was Vice-President of the Boston Latin School Association; a member of the Board of Overseers of Harvard College, and Secretary of the Board after 1849; a director in the Society for Promoting Theological Education; Corresponding Secretary of the Massachusetts Historical Society; and a member of various historical societies in other States. His heart was as warm as his head was bright. He was President of the Society for Promoting Christian Knowledge, Piety, and Charity; a member of the Massachusetts Congregational Charitable Society; a member of the Society for Propagating the Gospel among the Indians and Others in North America; and in all these offices he was a faithful servant. His library was handsomely stored with books, which were his delight, and his life was in full accord with his teaching. He was universally respected as a man, and much relied on as a pastor, and is an admirable example of that mingling of culture and character which marked the Unitarian ministers.

Dr. Young had humor also. He did enjoy a joke or a funny story. Just before his last sickness he was at a friend's house in Charlestown, making merry over a newspaper story of an old woman who complained of having the "brown critters." As he left the door to walk home he said, laughing: "I hope I shall not be attacked by the brown critters." Alas, he was. That night he took a cold which led to a fatal illness. Ten years after his death his meeting-house was taken down; George E. Ellis delivered the last sermon in it, and Dr. Frothingham wrote a hymn of parting, which is printed in the second series of the "Metrical Pieces."

WILLIAM PARSONS LUNT was also a power. He was not even so old as Alexander Young, when he died;

for he was born in 1805, and passed away at Akabàh, the ancient Ezion-Geber, on the eastern estuary at the head of the Red Sea, in 1857, within a month of fifty-one years of age. His grandfather, Henry Lunt, was a favorite officer of Paul Jones, who fought in the *Bonhomme Richard*, took part in the capture of the *Serapis*, and did good service in the war of the Revolution. The grandson had nothing of the soldier in his composition. Even on the field of theology he brandished no weapon, though filled with the earnest conviction that might have prompted him to strike down an enemy. He was a quiet, grave, silent man, introspective, undemonstrative, pensive; a man of brooding and apprehensive mind, of warm religious feeling, of fastidious intellectual proclivities. My father was very fond of him, and placed him among his " nine worthies " in the poem above referred to. Here is his description:

> A " rural bishop " now,
> With pale and furrowed brow,
> Draws up his chair beside my bed.
> The cloudy orb Saturn
> Drips from its leaden urn
> Its damps on his fine nature and clear head.

> Long will he silent sit,
> If no inspiring fit
> Rouse him to animated speech.
> His low unfrequent laugh,
> Half gay and plaintive half,
> Rolls like grave ocean toying with the beach.

> But give a quickening theme,
> And wake him out of dream,

And you shall feel what magic power
Of skilled melodious tongue,
And energies full strong,
Has genius in its high, ascendant hour.

Rhetor and poet too,
With taste severely true,
He writes for those who can judge well :—
But when his periods glance
With burning utterance,
Both taught and untaught feel the binding spell.

The fine hymn, the most beautiful in my opinion that N. L. Frothingham ever composed,

O God, whose presence glows in all,
Within, around us, and above,
Thy word we bless, thy name we call,
Whose word is Truth, whose name is Love,

was written for Mr. Lunt's ordination in New York, on the 19th of June, 1828; and the other hymn,

We meditate the day
Of triumph and of rest,
When, shown of God and shaped in clay,
The word was manifest !

was written for his installation at Quincy, June 3, 1835. Both, but particularly the latter, show the character of the Unitarian faith as respects the nature of Christ and the authority of the evangelical record. When Dr. Lunt died at Akabàh, on his way to the Holy Land, March 20, 1857, my father wrote the following touching " Lament : "

A LAMENT.

FOR REV. WILLIAM PARSONS LUNT, D.D.

A wail from beyond the desert !
A wail from across the sea !
   The home he left,
   Bereft, bereft,
For evermore must be.

As spread the heavy tidings,
How many a heart grows sore,
   That the eloquent grace
   Of that pensive face
And that mellow voice is o'er !

Alas for thee, O our brother !
And for this we sorrow most,
   That a spirit so fair
   Must be breathed out there,
On that stern Arabian coast ;—

That a life so all unforeign—
To faith and his country bound,—
   Turned dying eyes
   Upon Asian skies,
And dropped on Moslem ground.

Away for the Holy City
With pilgrim soul he trod ;
   But nearer at hand
   Must the pearl gates expand
Of the city new of God.

The judgment-peak of Sinai
Rose now in the homeward West ;
   Its shadows grim
   Had no terror for him
As he sank to his Christian rest.

But, oh, that the thoughtful scholar,—
His mind at its fullest noon,—
   That the preacher's tongue
   And the poet's song
Should pass away so soon !

Outside of his profession, in which he was most devoted, Mr. Lunt cultivated three fields, that of philosophy, that of history, and that of poetry. The first was foreshadowed in his "Forensic," on graduating from Harvard, the subject of which was, "Whether, in Point of Morality, the Truth be a Justification of an Alleged Libel on Private Character." Dr. Pierce said that it "bore the palm in speaking." It was further illustrated in a sermon preached at Jamaica Plain, on occasion of the installation of Rev. George Whitney, the subject of which was, "The Necessity of a Religious Philosophy"; in an address to the alumni of the divinity school, in 1852; and in the Dudleian lecture, delivered in 1855. This last was especially elaborate, and was even declared by a contemporary to be among the "most profound, brilliant, and masterly productions that have illustrated the highest of the sciences, in recent times."

His historical position, though he produced no extended work, is indicated by his high esteem among the members of the Historical Society, of which he was Corresponding Secretary.

His poetical leanings are indicated in his selection as poet of the Phi Beta Kappa Society, in 1837, on which occasion he gave the poem called "Psyche," afterwards printed in pamphlet form, and in a small volume published by his son, W. P. Lunt, "Gleanings," nine pieces from which are printed, by A. P. Putnam, in his book entitled "Singers and Songs of the Liberal Faith." These do not evidence an exalted range of genius, but show an ear for melody, a talent for rhyme, and an enkindled spirit. The author's type of theology comes out in them, as in all his of compositions. His was essentially an old-fashioned creed, built upon the text of Scripture, interpreted according to moral methods; a qualification of the Puritan theology, some of the tenets being discarded, as unauthorized by the Bible, or unsanctioned by natural feeling and conviction. "He was more ready to accept than anxious to define hallowed phrases. . . . His Puritan soul leaned back, as far as it dared, towards ancient formulas." His Dudleian lecture was a strong, impassioned plea for a spiritual basis for religion, "Natural" as well as "Revealed," taking as its subject, "The Province and Functions of Faith." So was the address to the alumni of the divinity school, on "The Faculty of Imagination in its Relations to Religion." Faith, he maintained, was independent of reason. Man had a religious nature, a spiritual vision, by virtue of which he could behold supersensual realities as plainly as the physical orb discerns the material world. The soul has laws of its own; and faith is one of its organic endowments. Science and sociology are excellent in themselves and to be heartily encouraged, but have nothing to do with religion. The method of Bacon was, on the whole, disastrous to faith, as awakening false expectations. Mr. Lunt's aim seems to have been the necessity of finding a philosophical ground that would justify the religious affections,—trust, veneration, charity, desire, aspiration, love of the infinite and eternal. Of theology, christology, bibliology, there was no mention. A wide distinction is drawn between Theology the *rationale* of religion and Religion itself. With critical discussions Mr. Lunt apparently gave himself little concern. He took the creed which his sect, his education, or his temperament provided. "Controversial religion was not to his liking. The biblical neologies of our new times were an offense if not an alarm to him. He held the literal Word reverently dear, although he endeavored to give it an expansive scope, and sought underneath it the most spiritual significances." This quotation from my father's tribute to him before the Historical Society, implies a dread of intellectual processes in religion, a distrust of the critical faculty, and a disposition to cling to the ancient standards of belief as far as his moral sentiments would allow. Secular themes, politics included, were banished from the pulpit, but the pastor did not refrain from expressing his mind on exciting topics of the day—spiritism and abolitionism for example,—and his opinion was by no means favorable to these, or any other disturbers of the peace.

This extreme conservatism, in a time of excitement, somewhat clouded the reputation of another admirable minister, and obscured his fine gifts. I refer to CHANDLER ROBBINS. It was his boast, during the civil war—a period of intense excitement and deep patriotic conviction throughout the community, when the pulpit even was expected to be sectional,—that neither sermon, prayer nor hymn had, in his church, reminded people of the strife. A painful incident, illustrating his habit of mind (one cannot call it apathy, or, on the other hand, an active hostility to the Northern cause, but rather a stubborn neutrality on political affairs), occurred at a meeting of the Historical Society, to which Mr. Robbins belonged. It was at one of the darkest episodes of the war. Defeat had followed defeat. The credit of the government was sinking. Conflict with England seemed imminent. An informal conversation on the situation went round the circle; Mr. Robbins joined in and criticised the proceedings at Washington, uttering sentiments that jarred on the ears of loyalists. One of the members, an old man, influential and honored, who had lost a son in battle, bore it as long as he could, chafing and fretting in his chair; but at length, unable to sit any longer, got up, faced the offender, shook his clenched fist at him, and ejaculated, "Then" (in the event of Northern overthrow and bankruptcy) "we will all go to hell together." Such was the temper of the people, and it required courage to confront it. This Mr. Robbins, be his conduct wise or foolish, did. It was the same spirit that called the outcry against Emerson's Divinity School address, a "vulgar clamor" and a "popular roar"; the same spirit that prompted him, after expressing the opinion that Mr. Parker should withdraw from the Unitarian Association when the general feeling was against him, to write Mr. Parker a letter, in which he said:

> I felt most deeply the delicacy and the hard trial of your situation, and am constrained to say that you sustained yourself nobly. It would have been unjust to you to have been less frank than we were.

The truth is, he was an inveterate peacemaker. His motto should have been: "Truth if possible, peace at any rate." No doubt his failure to uphold the Northern cause gave dissatisfaction to most of his people. Many left him; some disliked what they deemed his stubborness; and some were alienated by what they considered his arrogance and diplomatic astuteness ; to them he illustrated the "*perseverance of the saints.*" But he was much beloved. He was a minister born; a real priest and servant, with a dignified manner, a sweet, grave, sympathetic countenance, a deep, mellow voice, a simple, straightforward address, an evangelical appearance. His sermons were impressive, earnest, aimed directly at the conversion of souls to Christ. He was an excellent scholar in a rather distinguished class (that of 1829), and came out of the Divinity School in 1833. It should not be forgotten that, while in college, he showed remarkable courage in defending, alone, or almost alone, a classmate whom he believed to be wrongly accused of having betrayed a comrade to the faculty, and who in consequence was cut off from all intercourse with his companions; or that, while tutor in the Boston Latin School, he governed the boys habitually by force of character, resorting to corporal punishment once only, and then in a case of wanton cruelty, where the offense was against humanity. In the profession he succeeded R. W. Emerson and Henry Ware, Jr., who had his eye on him while yet a student, midway in his course at the Divinity School. The people, after such preaching, were delighted with him, gave him a unanimous call, and listened to him more than forty years. When he resigned, in 1874, he was the oldest-settled pastor in Boston.

Chandler Robbins was an admirable historical student; an enthusiastic chronicler of the old Boston story—the situation of his meeting-house, far down in Hanover Street, lending helps to that taste;—an antiquarian of no mean pretension; a poet too of rare fervor, one of his hymns,

> Lo the day of rest declineth;
> Gather fast the shades of night,

being a great favorite with worshippers of every Christian name; an essayist of elegance and skill. His researches were wide. I recollect his borrowing from my father Colebrook's volume on "The Philosophy of the Hindus" (in French). He was one of the "Nine Worthies" celebrated in verse:

> The calm expression of his air
> Is tender and yet strong.
> His fervors kindle into prayer
> And melt in sacred song.

Andrew P. Peabody, in his "Harvard Reminiscences," writes of him:

Dr. Robbins, several years before his death, met with an accident which was probably the cause of his loss of sight. From that time, darkness gathered over him by slow but sure stages, with no hopeful intermission. He worked while he was yet able cheerfully and earnestly; and when the shadows became so dense that he could guide neither his pen nor his step, he submitted, not as to the inevitable, but as to the hidden mercy of a loving Providence.

Another "worthy" who has, in his general reputation, suffered a little by his love for secular things —horses and festivities,—was SAMUEL KIRKLAND LOTHROP, the incumbent of the Brattle Street pulpit after John Gorham Palfrey and Edward Everett and Joseph Stevens Buckminster. He is justly described in the following lines from the poem that has been quoted so often:

>A frame of this world in a minister's gown
>And good in them both;—though a whip and athletic,
>In his whole sacred office devout, sympathetic.
>He is ready of speech and in fervor of spirit
>Tells his mind without caring to polish or shear it,
>Or to deck it out fine with rhetorical rays;
>It is good as it stands and quite sure of its praise,
>His genius runs prose, studies doctrines not graces,
>And sees always the facts in all manner of cases.
>O'er the highways of thought he moves wide and at ease,
>With no time for its nooks and small taste for its seas,
>And in Church and in State a conservative stout,
>Is "aye ready" for battle, with arms or without.
>A man of large nature, a man of affairs,
>Whose honest, brave soul in his manner he wears.
>Should you see him at times when his spirit mounts warm,
>With his hands in a clench and his brow in a storm,
>You might take him for some rough Dictator or other;
>But look at him close, he's all Christian and brother.

From this sketch it may safely be inferred that Dr. Lothrop's genius was more practical than speculative; that he was gifted with common-sense rather than with intellectual keenness, with human sagacity rather than with spiritual insight. According to my own observation, he was a model ecclesiastic, — not a priest of the Continental type, but an English bishop with the freedom of an American clergyman. With him the Church was an institution, and he was one of its appointed administrators. His fame as a preacher was not especially great. He was not reputed a prophet or seer. But he was exceedingly valuable as a minister. He had an imposing presence, a handsome countenance, a sonorous voice, a bluff, cordial manner, a hearty address, ready speech, a forcible pen. His dress was always in good order, his linen was of the whitest, his broadcloth of the blackest; but this was simply a personal, not an official, incident, an expression of his sense of neatness, of propriety, which would have appeared whatever his business was. His natural affections were warm, responsive, sensitive, as well abroad as at home, in his official as in his domestic relations. His conscientiousness was robust, his purpose humane, his aim, as a minister, high if not ideal. He was alive to the social privileges of his profession, the acquaintance of distinguished men, the easy access to the best society, the open door into the human breast on occasions of perplexity or sorrow, the demand for a clerical presence at civic or national observances; but he did not forget that he was a minister of the gospel, nor did he fail to impart some higher flavor to the festivities he engaged in. In the purlieus of the profession, to which, it is needless to say, he devoted himself most assiduously and acceptably, his industry was immense. He had the interests of education deeply at heart, served on committees, visited schools, wrote reports, offered suggestions, pressed reforms, was an active member of committees, and, in every way was most efficacious. His work at charitable organizations was incessant and laborious. He was president or secretary of innumerable societies, and he made his influence felt in them all. His interest in municipal, State, and national concerns was great and manifest. He was an ardent Whig, and let the citizen show through the clergyman's gown. The tributes paid to him after his death by ministers of renown spoke volumes in his praise. The respect and affection in which he was held were universally attested. Dr. Walker once said that if he were in need of pastoral offices there was no one he should go to sooner than to Dr. Lothrop. Wherever religion came into contact with human affairs, there he was at home. There he was most felicitous. I have heard him speak at weddings and at funerals, when it seemed that nothing could be better, and what he was

> in the dark Gethsemane
> Of pain, and midnight prayer,

the afflicted alone can tell.

After Dr. Lothrop's death, the Boston Association of Congregational Ministers, of which he was a leading man for half a century and Moderator nearly seventeen years, through a special committee paid him a warm tribute. Here is a part of it:

> No one among us was so thoroughly acquainted with the history, customs, and laws of our Congregational churches. And in the whole Congregational body not more than one or two others during the last forty years had made himself so intimately and personally acquainted with the wants and trials of ministers' bereaved families left widowed or fatherless in great destitution or with wholly inadequate means of support. But while the labors of his life reached through these wider relationships, he was most beloved and honored by those who knew him best. For they were made to feel as others could not, the Christian faith which bore him up under the heaviest bereavements, and the Christian kindliness and charity which "never failed," but kept the sweetness and the cheerfulness of his disposition untouched by the sorest trials and disappointments.

The temper of aggressive reform came in, so far as I can remember, with JOHN PIERPONT, of Hollis Street. Things invisible had not much interest for him. Things theological possessed little attraction. The bent of his mind was ethical rather than ethereal. His first profession was law, which he studied and practised, having been regularly admitted to the bar of Essex County. This not proving gainful, owing to the confusion incident to the War of 1812, he tried business, in Boston and Baltimore, but was not successful. Then, at the age of thirty-four, he entered the ministry, bringing an ability that had been trained in other fields, and a spirit of self-assertion such as the Boston clergy were not accustomed to. His interest in social reforms, especially in temperance, anti-slavery, prison discipline, began before he occupied the pulpit, and his outspokenness stirred up commotion in the tranquil community of believers, who were very mild in their reprobation of social abuses, and confined themselves to general moral exhortations. Discontent was expressed by him early, and in 1838 a controversy arose in the parish which led to the summoning of an ecclesiascal council to pronounce on the minister's conduct and to consider the relations between pastor and people. The result of the warfare was favorable to Mr. Pierpont, who gained the victory and thereupon resigned his place. The controversy is interesting here as illustrating the attitude of parishioners towards the minister at that time, the sentiment of the Boston Unitarian churches on the subject of social agitation, as well as the temper of Mr. Pierpont, which might have converted more had it been more persuasive. The truth is that he was fond of conflict. He was essentially a fighter. At the age of seventy-six he enlisted as chaplain in a Massachusetts regiment, and served as long as he could bear the fatigue, which was not long. Had he been interested in theology he would have been a controversialist, as, indeed, he was to a limited extent. Even his poetry has a martial ring, the strains of pure melody coming in like the sound of flutes in a military band. Some of the strains were exceedingly sweet, but the whole effect was stimulating, exciting, stirring, thrilling. A vein of heroism ran through the man, prompted him to take up unpopular causes that demanded courage, determination, vigor, in their champion, great activity of mind, force of will, executive talent. There was nothing original in his theological speculations, which were characterized rather by logical astuteness than by depth of thought. Spiritual insight was not his strong point. But, for the rest, he was a charming companion, hilarious, witty, full of anecdotes, an excellent scholar, according to the standard of the time, a wide reader, a man of large intelligence. The Unitarians of Boston were a little afraid of him, and shrank somewhat from his direct, incisive type of mind, but he was a valuable ally of their cause.

A very important and influential person was CONVERS FRANCIS, minister at Watertown and afterward professor in the Divinity School of Cambridge. I have elsewhere described him as " one of those rare men whom too few appreciate ; a liberal scholar, in the best sense of the phrase ; learned without pedantry ; open to the light from every quarter ; an enormous reader of books ; a great student of German philosophy and divinity, as very few at that time were. The newest criticism and speculation were on his table and in his mind. He was absolutely free from dogmatism,—the dogmatism of the liberal as well as the dogmatism of the conservative. The students of Cambridge, when he afterwards became professor in the Divinity School, found fault with him for being too " all-sided "—*non-committal*, they called it,—understanding neither his respect for their minds nor his reverence for the truth. He was a conscientious, natural eclectic, with as few intellectual prejudices as it is well possible to have. His lectures and sermons were full of suggestions, opening out lines of thought in every direction, eminently useful but eminently unsatisfactory to such as wanted opinions formulated for filing away. It was a happy, cordial, cheery mind, with extensive prospects from all the windows; he had an intellectual atmosphere it was a delight to inhale. Here were books without stint; here was a friend, an interpreter, and a sympathetic inquirer. Unfortunately, Dr. Francis was not possessed of force of will corresponding to all this wealth of equipment. He was not qualified to be a leader. But as a stimulator of thought, as a reservoir of extra-Christian erudition, his influence was felt through the denomination. He was one of the educators of Theodore Parker, and though he himself kept within denominational lines, and was never out of repute among his brethren, he was a herald of the new time. Parker wrote to Dr. Francis in 1842 : "No one who *helped* in my ordination will now exchange ministerial courtesies with me." Now Dr. Francis preached the sermon; yet Parker always maintained hearty relations with him, acknowledging the service he was rendering, and feeling sure of his substantial sympathy. Francis was at heart a transcendentalist and a reformer; a friend of Emerson and of Pierpont, but he could not break the ties that held him to his sect; he did not feel the necessity of doing so; his theory of influence recommending to him the wisdom of preserving existing relations. He said once that he who defies public opinion, like the man who spit in the wind, spits in his own face. His practice went with his teaching.

It is difficult to do full justice to such a man, to decide how much, in his conduct, was due to caution, and how much to impartiality. We can only classify him as an Erasmus; but Holbein's portrait of Erasmus would not answer for him at all. Instead of that calm, pale, passionless, thoughtful face, there is a full, ruddy countenance with an alert, eager expression, a look of inquiry, upward and forward turned as if expecting some new thing in the future, a jocund, cordial man with a vast deal of human nature in him. He was delighted when he could guide, advise, or help young men; was no recluse, and yet no man of the world, but a man of letters, hospitable, humane, with a real belief in mind, and the smallest faith in tradition of any sort. His writings were mainly of a historical or biographical character. The life of Rev. John Eliot, the Apostle to the Indians, in Sparks' "American Biography," was by him. The Massachusetts Historical Society honored him by a memoir. He was the most modest and diffident of men; too modest, too self-distrustful for immediate effect. Had he possessed more self-assertion, he would have been famous. Humility is an excellent quality, but it is not operative without a strong personality, as his was not. He had convictions, but no force to oppose them. He himself was a decided Unitarian of the ordinary school, and many passages in his sermons asserted his faith in the miraculous mission of Jesus, but his love of heroism, sincerity, truthfulness, led him to praise people whose views he dissented from. He respected mind. He was an inspirer of mind, and his influence in broadening the liberal pulpit was second to that of no one, as his successor, John Weiss, has said most eloquently and shown most convincingly. Whenever humanity was in question, as it was in the case of slavery, his sentiments were expressed firmly, courageously, and without regard to ancestors. Here there could not be two sides, nor were his opinions uttered in doubtful language. On this matter, he thought, the pulpit should be open for protest at all times.

Among the men who did honor to the Unitarian name was one not distinguished as preacher or writer, or for other shining gifts, but eminent for sheer goodness, and an admirable example of the piety that was, as often as in any sect, associated with the Unitarian belief. We must not forget NATHANIEL HALL, of Dorchester, an earnest, devoted Christian, a man without guile if there ever was one. There was nothing peculiar in his faith. At his ordination, July 16, 1835, E. B. Hall, of Providence, his brother, preached the sermon; Dr. Pierce offered the prayer; Dr. Palfrey gave the charge; George Putnam tendered the right hand of fellowship; Dr. Parkman made the address to the people : a pretty good evidence of conservative leanings. At the twenty-fifth anniversary of the settlement, July 16, 1860, there was nothing to indicate a departure from the accustomed ways of thinking in religion. At his death hearty tributes were paid by men like James F. Clarke, Andrew P. Peabody, George W. Briggs, James W. Thompson. But convictions are always radical, and here was a man of convictions. Mr. Hall began life as a clerk in a store; then he served as secretary in an insurance office. But neither of these pursuits satisfied the hunger of his soul. He had aspirations after an ideal calling. He entered the Divinity School at Cambridge, was graduated thence in 1834, and the next year was chosen colleague pastor with Thaddeus Mason Harris, in Dorchester, who resigned his charge in 1836. From that time Mr. Hall was the pastor, and remained in Dorchester till the end of his life, in 1875. He was a minister forty years, a most devoted one, the true friend of his people, taking a warm interest in their children, and concerning himself with all their spiritual affairs. He had a "true and effectual" calling from on high; was not pushed into the profession, or educated for it, or destined to it by ambitious relatives, but summoned to it by an inward impulse from heaven. He was all minister without the smallest reservation. The moral laws ran through his nature. Hence it was no violation of them but the simplest observance, when he gave expression to humane sentiments and tried to impress upon his congregation the claims of the slave. For there was an element of firmness in him, an unyielding persistency when conscience was involved, that would give way to no blandishments. His was not a pulpy goodness; there was *vir* in his virtue. There were verses about "righteousness" among the "Beatitudes," and these he heeded. Nor did he feel that he had discharged his whole duty to the Sermon on the Mount as long as these were silently omitted. Many were the beseechings, many the remonstrances, many the rebukes, many the desertions, many the departures from the meeting-house as the unwelcome message was delivered, but no effect was produced. There was organized opposition, still the preacher persevered, retaining the cordial respect of his opponents. For nothing personal mingled with his admonitions. There was no invective, no rancor, no sarcasm, no innuendo. The exposition was calm, the argument unimpassioned, the appeal dignified. Nothing inflammatory tainted the discourse. The moral force was felt through the sermon even by objectors, who sometimes expressed regret at their rudeness. To the charge of introducing politics into the pulpit he replied:

> The pulpit stands before the community as the visible representative, the public organ, the accredited voice of its religion. Should it fail of bearing testimony, openly and

unequivocally against this wrong, what would be the unauthorized inference from such failure,—the natural language of it? Would it not be, that religion, as such, had no rebuke for it,—had nothing to do with it? . . . An impression, I learn, exists with some of you, that, in allowing the anti-slavery enterprise to find continued advocacy in this pulpit, I have been untrue to some expressions in the sermon at my return [from Europe, where he had been],—expressions which were understood, most strangely, to involve a confession of regret at my past course in relation to this enterprise, and the avowal of a purpose to avoid its repetition. I desire to say, that not the slightest shadow of such an idea ever entered my mind. No! No! Among the things in the past which I regret, and they are many, this, believe me, is not one. Among the resolutions with which I crossed anew the threshold of my work, there was none of desistance from the advocacy of this holy cause. Its summoning trump, heard long years ago,—heard, and, I bless God, heeded,—wakes still its echoes in my soul; and when I shall willingly be disobedient to it may the earth miss me, and its befriending turf conceal me! Circumstances require that I should be explicit in this matter. This, therefore, I desire to say, that I stand here in perfect freedom, or I stand not here at all; and that, in the exercise of that freedom, among the subjects that will be introduced here, is that of righteousness in its application to the great sin of the nation, —to American slavery.

To the question "what good will such discussion do?" Mr. Hall made answer:

I do not know; I do not care to know. Ask Him who formed the soul for truth, to find therein its sustenance and salvation, and whose kingdom is to come in the world only through his blessing upon the spoken and manifested truth. Ask him who "for this end was born, and for this cause came into the world, that He might bear witness to the truth," and who bore witness to it against scoff and sneer, the frown of power, and the threatening of hate, in the sublime faith that it would win for itself, at length, a universal triumph. Ask the thousands who, in a like faith, have lived and died for it,— lived in persecution, died in martyrdom ; scattering as they went, on the world's bleak waysides, its celestial seeds, to spring and bloom above their graves.

These are touching words of deep, unselfish conviction, such as none but an heroic, trusting soul could speak. A moral power at least must have gone out of them, and reached the heart. Such a power did throb in many consciences that could not give it such eloquent expression. Unitarianism certainly lent itself to like persuasions. The cardinal doctrine of the essential uprightness of human nature, of the native capacity of man—that is, of *development* instead of *conversion*, encouraged efforts to remove restrictions, to take away social barriers, to emancipate mankind from needless oppression, and give people a chance to expand. We saw this result in Channing, Emerson, Ripley, Pierpont, Parker, Clarke, Hall, Francis, Weiss, Wasson, Ellis, Willson, and many another. On the other hand, Unitarianism was the religion of the educated, the refined, the scholarly, the wealthy, the leaders of society. Great merchants, politicians, statesmen, judges were apt to be members of Unitarian congregations. This influence was strongly conservative of the existing order, and threw the weight of public opinion against agitation or reform. Of course, this power was felt most in Boston and the neighborhood; in remote country towns and villages it was hardly perceptible, so that it required a good deal of courage to resist the ruling sentiment and maintain the independence of the pulpit when it was measured by the respectability of the pews.

Then there were differences of temperament, and of culture, more pronounced among the educated than among the unlettered, as they probed issues deeper, had a greater variety of interests, possessed a more complicated individuality. Some ministers frankly defended slavery, claiming, with Edward Everett (a Unitarian by the way), that it was "a condition of life, as well as any other to be justified by morality, religion, and international law." Such men did not have in view the principle which insisted on freedom as a condition of *moral* enfranchisement wholly without regard to the misery of the slaves. Others were quite unconcerned about the matter, holding that it was none of their business, and were absorbed in matters close at hand. The "violence" of the Abolitionists, their denunciation of all slave-holders, offended the daintier or more scrupulous minds. Many contended that their duty was to their churches, and that this duty was confined to the task of building up in them a Christian character, leaving to them the details of conduct. A few were timid, but not many. The charge of hypocrisy cannot be sustained. And certainly it is not for ordinary mortals to blame those who could not withstand the steady, universal pressure of the distinguished, the wise, and the respected, whose judgment in other affairs was supreme. None but heroic souls can do that. We may classify them, but we may not denounce them. Let us honor the faithful; let us leave the unfaithful to their consciences.

This was the old quarrel, handed down to the Whigs and Democrats of a later day from the Federalists and Republicans of an earlier period. In 1801, Theodore Dwight, in an oration delivered at New Haven, July 7th, said,—I quote from Henry Adams' "History of the United States," vol. i., p. 225 :

> The great object of Jacobinism, both in its political and moral revolution, is to destroy every trace of civilization in the world, and to force mankind back into a savage state . . . That is, in plain English, the greatest villain in the community is the fittest person to make and execute the laws. . . . We have now reached the consummation of democratic blessedness. We have a country governed by blockheads and knaves; the ties of marriage, with all its felicities, are severed and destroyed ; our wives and daughters are thrown into the stews ; our children are cast into the world from the breasts and forgotten ; filial piety is extinguished, and our surnames, the only mark of distinction among families, are abolished. Can the imagination paint any thing more dreadful on this side hell?

Rev. Joseph Buckminster, of Portsmouth, New Hampshire, father of Joseph Stevens Buckminster, said in a sermon on Washington's death :

> I would not be understood to insinuate that contemners of religious duties [he had Jefferson in mind], and even men void of religious principle, may not have an attachment to their

country and a desire for its civil and political prosperity ; . . . but by their impiety . . . they take away the heavenly defence and security of a people, and render it necessary for him who ruleth over the nations in judgment to testify his displeasure against those who despise his laws and contemn his ordinances. (Adams, i., 81.)

His son, probably, shared his opinion ; for a writer in the *Boston Anthology*, January, 1807, thus expressed the sentiments of the literary class :

We know that in this land, where the spirit of democracy is everywhere diffused, we are exposed, as it were, to a poisonous atmosphere, which blasts every thing beautiful in nature, and corrodes every thing elegant in art. (Adams, i., 99.)

Enough account is not generally made of the purely social element in the opposition of the Unitarian ministers, as a rule, to the Abolitionists. They were gentlemen; they occupied a high position in the community; they belong to a privileged order; they were inclined to honor great people. It was, in this respect, unfortunate that they had so many eminent men in their congregations. Such characters as Daniel Webster, Edward Everett, Amos A. Lawrence, could not but influence the opinions of those who lived out of the political and commercial world. Ordinary modesty would have prompted an attitude of deference, and a most extraordinary moral conviction was required to resist their knowledge and power. Saints might have withstood them; heroes might; but heroes and saints were few, and the city clergymen who could rise above social considerations deserve far more credit than they got. They were possessed of remarkable courage. With the solitary exception of Wendell Phillips, who was regarded as an aristocratic demagogue, the Abolitionists were poor, humble, despised people, of no influence; men one could not ask to dine, who were not respected "on change," who had no place in halls of legislation, who were the natural antagonists of the refined and well esteemed. It is quite possible that, if the situation had been reversed, the Unitarian ministers would have been more anti-slavery than they were, for they had humanity enough to temper social prejudice, but not enough to surmount it. As it was, they were staunch Whigs, hated the very name of Jefferson, dreaded Democracy, abhorred what they called Jacobinism, which seemed to them allied with "infidelity," and were strenuous upholders of Union and peace. The following lines of my father on Daniel Webster, written at sunset, October 22, 1852, show the bent of their feeling.

> Sink, thou Autumnal Sun!
> The trees will miss the radiance of thine eye,
> Clad in their Joseph-coat of many a dye;
> The clouds will miss thee in the fading sky;
> But now in other scenes thy race must run,
>   This day of glory done.
>
> Sink, thou of nobler light!
> The land will mourn thee in its darkening hour;
> Its heavens grow gray at thy retiring power,
> Thou shining orb of mind, thou beacon-tower!
> Be thy great memory still a guardian might,
>   When thou art gone from sight.

Longfellow's praise of the Union, at the end of his poem, "The Building of the Ship," is in point, as illustrating the faith of a prominent layman.

> Thou too, sail on, O Ship of State!
> Sail on, O Union, strong and great!
> Humanity with all its fears
> Is hanging breathless on thy fate!
> Our hearts, our hopes are all with thee,
> Our hearts, our hopes, our prayers, our tears,
> Our faith triumphant o'er our fears,
> Are all with thee, are all with thee!

This was in them a faith, a real faith, a faith in civilization, progress, amity, friendship, humanity, the interests of the intellectual world, the future destinies of society. The Union meant power of conscience, the sway of moral sentiment, the predominance of the best. Love for it was, by no means, inconsistent with a sincere detestation of slavery, but slavery was perhaps hated less than Union was loved. Moreover, the Union of the States was regarded as the ultimate pledge of the extinction of slavery, as the civil war afterwards proved it was, for emancipation was an episode in the attempt to save the Union by Mr. Lincoln. And then, too, slavery was honestly supposed to be really on the decline though apparently increasing in power, while other evils as great as slavery, if not greater,—evils inseparable from anarchy,—seemed sure to follow upon disintegration. The demand of the Abolitionists for disunion made them peculiarly offensive to these patriots. The demand might, in their judgment, be logical enough, but against it were sentiment and charity and the forces of civilization, which, though it worked slowly, worked surely and beneficently. The process of elevating any portion of mankind was long, requiring much patience, and they who thought to effect it at once by an ethical impulse, fell into a most disastrous misconception. Longfellow's close intimacy with Charles Sumner attested his own anti-slavery feeling, and doubtless he believed that a general moral sentiment that would ensure final emancipation must somehow result from the influence of Northern ideas, reinforced by principle and rendered humane by pity. Thus a hearty belief in the future of the Union, bringing into exercise, as it was confidently supposed, all the elements of the highest attainment, promised a bloodless solution of the problem of negro servitude. It was thought that the Abolitionists did more harm than good, inasmuch as they discouraged the finest sentiments of humanity,—peace, charity, brotherly kindness, hope of progress,—and erected a single trait, moral indignation, above every grace of cultivated character inculcated in the New Testament. It would be wiser, some maintained, to buy the slaves outright, than to risk an agitation that would certainly alienate friendly feeling and render remonstrance unavailing, even if it did not provoke recrimination and hatred. Such was the faith of some very trustful souls.

I have said that the social element entered largely

into the Unitarian opposition to the Abolitionists. It was, in great measure, responsible for the dislike of democratic institutions. This dislike was very old, and had a most respectable parentage in Massachusetts; John Winthrop, the predecessor of Washington, and men of his stamp, distrusted them. In a letter summarized by Winthrop himself at the end of his history, and quoted by Roger Williams, he said: "The best part of a community is always the least, and of that least part the wiser are still less"; a maxim which is true enough, and would be decisive if the question concerned an aristocracy and not a republic, in which all the people, cultivated or uncultivated, must have charge of their own interests as governors of themselves. "Civil liberty," he writes in his speech on government, "is liberty to do that only which is good, just, and honest"; which reminds one of Milton's lines about those

> That bawl for freedom in their senseless mood
> And still revolt when truth would set them free.
> License they mean when they cry liberty;
> For who loves that, must first be wise and good.

How often have I heard those lines cited, as if the truism they contained settled the whole matter of freedom!

The association of the highest order of virtue with aristocratic leanings rendered the sentiment exceedingly seductive. The conservatives, as a rule, were high-toned men, though not all high-toned men were conservative. They relied on character; they were friends of education, instruction, knowledge. They respected excellence, and it seemed to them certain that obscure men, tied down to sordid needs, could not have lofty minds—must be fanatics. If Daniel Webster had been mean, if Edward Everett had been base, if William Prescott had been servile, or George Ticknor a scoundrel, the case might have been altered. As it was, "righteousness and peace kissed each other." Doyle's remark is justified that Winthrop's blameless integrity disarmed suspicion of some of his opinions.

In the meantime it should be noticed that the criticism of motives was as generous as it was infrequent. There was a cordial fellowship between those who held the most opposite opinions on these and other questions of applied morals. It was taken for granted that the fundamental principles of humanity were cherished by every preacher of righteousness; that all were lovers of their fellow-men; that each was honest in his conception of duty; that there was room for different readings of the minister's calling. There was little or no jealousy, and absolutely no ill-will. In a fraternity as large and comprehensive, where the purely literary spirit was so prominent, and the temptations to worldliness were so numerous, this is saying a good deal.

But in the case of Mr. Hall it was felt that opposition to slavery was simply and wholly an act of duty, a part of his religion, and was respected accordingly. His sense of humanity was outraged by the system; his moral principle was shocked by its injustice; his conception of Christianity as a religion of brotherly love was insulted; personally, in his soul, he felt the disgrace and shame of such an institution. His opposition to slavery was not a matter of temper, or of temperament, it was a matter of principle. If he had considered social or professional consequences, he would have held his peace. But a conviction like his could not regard consequences, could not see them. His was a real call to the ministry. It was the dream of his youth, a genuine hunger of the heart. Necessity compelled him to earn money in business, but destiny decreed that his early longing should be carried out. The firm he was first connected with, at the age of 15, failed when he had been there a year and a half, so that he was thrown out of employment. The second, a ship-chandlery, on Long Wharf, was closing up, and his time there was lost, at any rate, for the work was entirely uncongenial. Then he became secretary of an insurance office, but the labor was exhausting, the associations were any thing but encouraging, and the old desire returned in its original force. He saved up a little money—enough, he thought in his ignorance,—went away, much against the wishes of his parents and friends, and began to study with a brother who was a clergyman at Northampton. The brother had to go off for his health, and Nathaniel went with him. Here was more precious time lost; the scanty means were diminished; and the prospect seemed as far off as ever. But he persevered in the face of all discouragements, including the temporary displeasure of an uncle (P. C. Brooks), whose wealth had been an important aid to him. It was a long experience of patience, and courage, and aspiration, and devotion to an ideal. That devotion conquered at last, and he soon vindicated the truth as well as the fervency of his longing. His uncle was by and by brought around, and became the most efficient of helpers. How he dared to enter the Divinity School was a marvel, but he did. It is needless to say that he worked hard. For the larger part of three years he boarded himself at an expense of seventy-five cents a week. It is a wonder that he lived to be 70 years old. He left the Divinity School in 1834, and in 1835 was ordained, his inward preparation making amends for the lack of college training.

A conviction of the reality of spiritual things was the strong feature of his character. This rendered business of every kind distasteful to him, and obliged him to abandon all his situations; this carried him to the Divinity School and kept him there in spite of his hardships and insufficient training; this ensured him an honored place in the ministry; this gave him firmness of resistance when it became necessary to assert his anti-slavery convictions; this confirmed his gentleness when that was of first importance to hold the affections of his people, and won over many of his opponents; this held him close to the bosom of his brethren; this made him expansive in his sympathies. For the scientific, critical, speculative aspects of belief, he cared little; for the humane, spiritual aspects of it he cared much. Hence his large tolerance of men whose opinions he could not share,—men like Parker for instance,— and hence his disposition to penetrate beneath the letter of Scripture to its inner moral significance, a disposition that might be dangerous when not guarded by strong good-sense. His natural conscience revolted at once, without a struggle, from the doctrine of Calvinism, so that he was always a Unitarian at heart; controversy was no more distasteful to him than it was unnecessary; and it cost him no effort to be generous. He was a born Christian in the best sense of the word, humble, self-forgetting, devout, with self-renouncing, unambitious temper, simple-minded, pure-souled, loving to serve; no priest by profession, but a minister of the gospel, and nothing else.

I say all this partly in order to show how completely spontaneous Unitarianism may be, and partly to vindicate its essential religiousness when relieved of its dogmatic character. It can produce saints, and does when allowed full scope. The reproach that it is an intellectual system purely, is entirely removed by an experience like Nathaniel Hall's. Here, at least, was a man who did not have to be apologized for; who was not merely true to his convictions, but whose convictions were worth being true to; a man in whom the want of an intellectual brilliancy was a positive advantage as throwing into strong relief the spiritual elements of character. Of course it will be objected that, in this case, the native temperament fell in with the superinduced creed. But this, too, is an advantage, inasmuch as the whole man was exhibited, and the fitness of the creed to a positive, strong disposition is demonstrated. The absence of conflict, where the faith is sincere, is a commendation of the faith; and when the disposition, coming first, forms its belief, the belief is apt to be vital, acting as a reinforcement to stimulate what is already powerful. Much has been said, and with great show of reason, in behalf of the victory of faith over desire, but, after all, time and strength are spent in such moral conflict, and, if the victory be won finally, the result is the same as when there is no conflict at all, while the vigor of the best years is secured to religion. There is no foundation equal to that of goodness, and if religion builds the superstructure according to its own design, we are sure of a perfect edifice. Of course religion must do the building. One cannot live in even the most admirable cellar. But religion, to be complete, needs a foundation, and a firm foundation is more to be desired than an unsound one; an adequate foundation is especially desirable, instead of one that must be made over anew out of the miserable materials of a disordered nature that has no ready conscience, no sensitive heart, and no loyal will.

Most of these men were writers in the *Christian Examiner*, many of them often, and at length, giving their best work to it, and elaborating for it their ripest ideas. The *Examiner* was, on the whole, a perfect representative of the body—broad, free, elastic, undogmatical, unecclesiastical, literary. It was not a money-making magazine, trading on the popular reputations of distinguished men, but a real organ of thought, and its final decease was a serious loss, not to the denomination alone, but to the cause of enlightened mind. The best scholars conducted it, the best writers contributed to it. It lived on the vitality of the Unitarian movement, and it died when that movement became less distinctive, more social and more secular. Its history shows its force. In the true sense of the word, it was a development from the *Monthly Anthology*, a magazine half theological and half literary, the mouthpiece of the Anthology Club, a coterie made up of Unitarian ministers and laymen. The pastor of the First Church, William Emerson, was a member; the pastor of the Brattle Street Church, J. S. Buckminster, the brilliant preacher and talker, the enthusiast for intellectualism in its fullest extent, as well Greek as Hebrew, classical as biblical; the pastor of the New South, S. C. Thacher; Joseph Tuckerman, the philanthropist; John Thornton Kirkland, of whom nothing more need be said here; several lawyers and physicians, afterwards eminent; all together the ornaments of society, the most accomplished men of letters of the time, belonged to the Anthology Club. Their journal lasted from 1804 till 1811. This was succeeded in 1812 by the *General Repository and Review*, a bolder magazine, edited by Andrews Norton aided by Buckminster and Edward Everett. The *Repository* was more decidedly anti-trinitarian. Mr. Norton's "Defence of Liberal Christianity" appeared there. But both of the magazines were too intellectual for the people, and died from lack of support. The confidence of the few would not make a substitute for the purses of the many. The motto, "Nec temerè nec timidè," was a good one, and it was acted up to, but it failed to catch the popular imagination.

The *Christian Disciple* was the next effort. Its aim was to speak the truth in love, but at first, under the conduct of Noah Worcester, later known as the "Friend of Peace," there was so much love in it that the edge of the sword of truth was not felt. It began in 1813. In 1819, under another editor, it became more aggressive; still it was not fierce enough for the demand after 1823, and the *Examiner* followed in 1824, working on similar lines with the *Disciple*, and preserving the same spirit of charity, but laying sharper emphasis on theological ideas. The revolt against orthodoxy had been in a great measure anonymous, and the defiance of a few up to the "Controversy" which may be said to have begun with Dr. Channing's sermon at Baltimore in 1819. The *Disciple* had barely recognized the change that was going on in the current belief, and had not breathed the word "Unitarianism." Henceforth a new faith was to be assumed. The *Disciple* had, on the whole, been less pugnacious than the *Repository*, and the *Anthology*, while it dealt some heavy blows, was careful not to commit individuals to "liberal" opinions. It would not be easy, perhaps it would be impossible, to trace the gradual opening of more extended views in philosophy and religion through the pages of the *Examiner*, so much depends on the genius or state of the mind of editors, and on the questions that arise as years go on; but it is certain that thoughts were enlarged as the numbers multiplied. The *Christian Examiner* illustrated the new Unitarian mind from 1824 till 1869; and, as we know, that mind was continually expanding. Then it died, and *Old and New*, the very name of which indicates a fresh departure towards inclusiveness, took its place. This also came to an end in 1872, being superseded by secular magazines.

In 1829 an effort was made to reanimate the *Examiner*. As a change was deemed expedient, a meeting was held at the house of Dr. Channing; a new society was formed, and other arrangements for publication entered upon. It was agreed that "the general views of religion presented in the work shall correspond to those which have hitherto appeared in the *Christian Examiner*. It shall be a main object of the publication, in treating any book or subject which has a bearing on religion or morals, to present those considerations respecting it, which would suggest themselves to the mind of an enlightened Christian. The work shall be characterized by openness, fearlessness, and moderation in the expression of opinion on any topic of public interest, not flattering popular prejudices nor accommodating itself to them." That is to say, that the *Examiner* was to be a pronounced vehicle of liberal Christianity; and the declaration that it was to "contain an account of the most important and interesting new publications, and thus give a general view of the progress of literature and the popular sciences and of new discoveries of general interest," proves an intention to interpret this liberality generously, in accordance with the laws of reason. It has been faithful to this resolution. Theodore Parker, in 1839, wrote in his journal: "I have just finished a review of Strauss for the *Examiner*. I could not say all I would say from the standpoint of the *Examiner*—for this is not allowable,—but the most the readers of that paper will bear." But Mr. Parker's article was accepted, as of course it would be, if it was simply an account of Strauss' position; there was no reason *in that* why it should not appear in the *Examiner*.

The society first assumed a regular form on January 27, 1829, by choosing its officers. Andrews Norton was chosen President; F. W. P. Greenwood, Secretary; Nathan Hale, Treasurer. The Publication Committee consisted of James Walker, John G. Palfrey, and F. W. P. Greenwood. Among the subjects mentioned as suitable for treatment, illustrating the wide scope of discussion, were "Lyceums," "Our National Union," "Dugald Stewart," "Books in Modern Greek," "Lectures at the London University," "The Tariff," "Railroads," "Duties of the Medical Profession to Society," "Lotteries," "Poor Debtors," "Theatres," "American Literature." In 1830 it was decided by general opinion that Mr. Jefferson's political principles and character were not properly subject to discussion in such a work. F. W. P. Greenwood and James Walker became editors in 1831. Mr. Walker resigned as editor at the close of 1836. In 1839 William Ware was appointed editor. Alvan Lamson and E. S. Gannett succeeded him in 1843. George Putnam and George E. Ellis assumed the charge in 1849. In 1857, on the resignation of Mr. Ellis, the editorship was transferred to F. H. Hedge, and Edward E. Hale was associated with him. Mr. Hale resigned in 1861. In 1863 the society was dissolved by its own vote.

But the *Examiner* did not die. There was an enthusiasm for it that encouraged its friends in spite of financial difficulty. The property, such as it was, at once was made over to Rev. Thomas B. Fox, and he, with Rev. Joseph H. Allen, an indefatigable and laborious man, carried it on for several years, until it finally went to New York, fell into Henry W. Bellows' hands, and died. Mr. Allen conducted the review with a vigor and force that should have ensured success, if moral or intellectual qualities alone could, and after its cessation its friends, as if unwilling to yield to circumstances, started *Old and New*, in the hope that, under another name and with more secular attractions, it might renew its career. But notwithstanding Edward E. Hale's prodigious efforts and singular genius, the competition of other magazines was too much for it, and this, too, had a short existence of a few years only. The loss of such a journal as the *Examiner*, so able, so independent, so dispassionate, so unpartisan, so high-spirited, so consecrated to lofty ideas, was, as has been said, sorely regretted. True, it was always "Christian," but with such a large and generous interpretation that none save aggressive minds could feel the limitation. The best essays of W. E. Channing, James Walker, F. W. P. Greenwood, Orville Dewey, Andrews Norton, appeared there; the keenest criticism of books and opinions, the most thoughtful consideration of social problems. The entire series is a treasury of enlightened discussion, in which every subject that concerned men twenty years and more ago was seriously dealt with.

The literary influence of the *Examiner* was very great, although impalpable, as the atmosphere is. Its editors were scholars as well as thinkers; men of letters as well as divines, being familiar with the choicest writing, and insisting on a rational presentation of ideas, the intellectual laws and not dogmatic prejudices being respected. One cannot think without grateful admiration of the leaders in this enterprise, the earnest, convinced men, who gave time and strength to a reasonable revision of their religion. Names that are illustrious lent their radiance to those pages. Names that are unknown are embalmed there. When Mr. Allen took it,—his connection began in 1857, under Dr. Hedge, and gradually assumed more responsible proportions, till in 1863 he became sole editor and joint proprietor, continuing managing editor from 1865 till 1870, when the *Examiner* was merged in *Old and New*, —a younger class of men naturally came to the front, other issues were raised, and the character of the original review was slightly altered. Finally, on the decease of *Old and New*, there existed no organ of Unitarianism save the *Christian Register* the wide-known weekly paper which continues its liberalizing work, takes an independent stand, maintaining the broadest rationalism consistent with faith, and does its best to make up for the loss of the larger magazine.

IX.

THE BOSTON ASSOCIATION OF CONGREGATIONAL MINISTERS.

In 1860 Dr. Gannett thus described this conference:

Thirty-six years ago I met in this ministerial circle Dr. Porter, of Roxbury, wise, calm, sententious, from whose remark in one of our discussions I have tried to draw comfort ever since : " A minister should feel that he does no small amount of good in preventing the evil which would show itself if he were not in his place " ; Dr. Freeman, sensibly feeling the infirmities of age, but with a mind that years had only ripened, and a heart that never grew old ; Dr. Harris, of Dorchester, the faithful pastor and diligent student, sensitive, tender, and devout ; Dr. Pierce, of Brookline, always laden with facts, and always prompt with kind greetings ; Dr. Gray, who never dreaded the truth, but who loved harmony more than controversy ; Dr. Tuckerman, the minister of Chelsea, where he was preparing himself for the work that has spread his name through Christendom ; Dr. Richmond, gentle, urbane, modest ; Dr. Channing, who came to the meetings but seldom, but when present showed his interest in our purposes ; Dr. Lowell, always genial, always faithful, whose affectionate notes from his retirement at Elmwood show an interest which he has never lost in us. Of the men whom I accounted venerable as I looked on their grave faces and matured forms he alone remains. Of those who stood on a lower plane of age, but were regarded with little less of timid respect, one still gives us the light of his benignant countenance and the warmth of his cordial sympathy (Dr. Frothingham), though he has chosen to withdraw himself from our professional labors. Parkman was with us, full of terse sayings, and often disturbing me by a quotation from Scripture so apt that its pertinency made its irreverence ; Mr. Pierpont, earnest, ready, eloquent ; Henry Ware, whose place in our hearts is indicated by the constancy with which we spoke of him under his Christian name, and who could always be relied on for co-operation in every measure that aimed at personal or social improvement; Palfrey, then as industrious in his clerical service, and as upright in his purposes, as he has been laborious and consistent ever since ; Greenwood, delicate in health, sweet in temper, spiritual in his tastes, refined in his habits ; Walker, steady in mind, as true as steel, and as fraternal as he was honest, he who is now the candid hearer where he was once the careful preacher ; and others who took a less frequent or less earnest part in our meetings.

These meetings were held then, as now, twice every month, at our several houses. We were more punctual in our attendance than of late years, and came together, as it seemed to me, rather for friendly conversation than for deliberate discussion. Dr. Lowell and Dr. Pierce were the first to appear ; and more ecclesiastical views and more of the results of our professional experiences were exchanged between us than at present. The older members preferred the agreeable and desultory talk, which was a refreshment after the exercises of Sunday ; while the younger brethren made successive—and successful—attempts to turn the afternoon to a more profitable use.

The most distinct among the impressions which I retain of the years in which I was one of the younger members of this body relates to the character of our intercourse with one another. It was free, frank, cordial, and healthy to a most remarkable degree. Difference of age, of opinion, of situation, produced no estrangement or coolness. Discussions in which we maintained opposite views caused no heart-burning or ungenerous criticism. The playful remark, often bearing a sharp point, or the severe dissent honestly expressed, if it inflicted a momentary pain, only became the occasion of a more hearty confidence. Perhaps distance throws a false light over those days; but I love to look back on the mutual respect and bold trust which marked our social relations at that time as almost without parallel among ecclesiastical men.

This encomium is well deserved. The same cordiality existed in my day, and was largely due, as it appeared to me, to the social character of the gatherings, and the personal relation that existed among the gentlemen. They were not professional assemblies which put people on their guard, and gave an official tone to the words spoken. The temper of the individual men alone came out, and this could easily be allowed for. In fact differences did but lay emphasis on individuality, thus rendering the meetings interesting. There could not well be debate, in other than friendly fashion. The custom of presenting some subject by the chairman ensured pertinency and gravity, while the rule of calling on each one present for an expression of mind guaranteed a complete exhibition of view. The subject was always one of general concern, not sectarian usually, and the talk was unembarrassed, friendly, and fearless. The meeting was in private parlors. The hour before tea was spent in pleasant chat; the hour after tea was devoted to the serious concerns of the evening, or the other way. At all events part of the time was set apart for personal conversation. Under such an arrangement much will depend on the disposition, or habit of thought, or interest, of him who conducted the meeting. If that was close and logical the spirit of the proceedings would show it. If these were discursive or vague, the tendency would be exhibited. For example, Dr. Gannett wanted sharp definition; Dr. Frothingham, on the other hand, was better pleased by inclusive statements. The inclination of the former may be illustrated by the following incident. It was customary for the entertainer to open the meeting with prayer. Dr. Gannett's petition was long and comprehensive, including the members, their churches, the sick and bereaved, the outside world, the heathen and all who came within the range of the gospel. Dr. Bartol followed him. With upturned face and open eyes and hands outstretched to heaven, he simply said: "O Lord, we are here;" as much as to say, "we are waiting for a blessing." The old and the new could hardly be more sharply contrasted. As regards my father, I find this entry in Dr. Gannett's diary, which I take from Wm. C. Gannett's admirable biography of his father.

Ministers' Association meeting at Rev. Dr. Nath. Frothingham's. Large meeting—thirty there,—several not of the Association. Subject of discussion, "Our Differences." Dr. Frothingham said we were all Rationalists, all Naturalists, all Supernaturalists; defining these terms in his own way, and having acknowleged and spoken of a centre and two wings in our body.

It may be safely assumed that Dr. Frothingham's "definitions" were, in the eyes of a strict logician, no definitions at all. He was not one who looked at things through the medium of logic; he was rather disposed to reconcile divergences than to create them; to take large interpretations; to regard systems of opinion through sentiment and the constructive reason; to study the things that made for peace. There was this difference of temperament, and the charm of the Association was the free play of this difference. The men made the friendliest observation of one another. There was no official responsibility for opinion, and the personality could come out without reserve. It was very different from a public demonstration, where men represented, not themselves alone, but their social position, or their ecclesiastical situation. Here they could let themselves out with no danger of being misrepresented or compromised. Hence its popularity with those whose minds were full of ideas that could not be publicly communicated. As the meetings always were held on Monday, when ministers usually felt exhausted from the services of the previous day, the members, more or less dulled, preferred, in the main, light and easy conversation; and, as the intervals between the meetings were mostly, sometimes entirely, spent in parish duties, the talk turned naturally on parochial affairs. But the topics of discussion were varied, and the talk had a wide range. The conferences were often brilliant, and when men who read a great deal, thought much, and had a gift of speech, took a leading part, the listening was very agreeable; for many of the clergymen possessed wit and knowledge and fine perception. On occasions of excitement, as during the Parker controversy, which implicated both theological and personal questions, the words flew thick and fast from nearly all lips. Then the most silent had something to say about the duties of the profession. The Parker episode, in January, 1843, was disagreeable, for personal feeling was as much enlisted as dogmatical dissent. As the chairman, Dr. Frothingham, said, this was an "association of brethren," a fellowship, and that made the situation the more difficult. Had it been simply a theological club, the matters in dispute might have been easily disposed of. Even stiff conservatives, like Chandler Robbins, were touched, and extended a friendly hand to the heresiarch; and many a man who disagreed with Mr. Parker in doctrine, yet who loved him as a man, wished him to remain in the fraternity. The mixture of tenets with affection was, in the main, answerable for the dilemma. Fortunately such confusion was rare. The intercourse was of the heart, and disputation was foreign to the purpose of the conference, a circumstance that should be borne in mind by those who would understand the proceedings on the occasion in question. Action was forced upon the body, and action quite inconsistent with its original constitution. Hence the apparent severity of some, and the seeming generosity of others whose real opinions were covered up beneath personal kindness.

The institution was old as we estimate age. Dr. John Pierce, who was an authority on dates, mentioned Rev. Simeon Howard, D.D., as finishing a seventeen years' term as Moderator, in 1804. Dr. Pierce was himself "approbated" by the Association to preach, on February 22, 1796. The Association may be supposed to have been of English origin, as the Thursday Lecture was. It is said to have come from Bodmin, in Cornwall, and to have been introduced into this country by Rev. Charles Morton, who was a member of it both in the old home and the new, the only man of whom this can be affirmed; but it must have been much older, as it was objected to by Roger Williams on the ground of its restrictive tendencies. Mr. Morton was a graduate of Oxford, and rector of Blissland, in Cornwall. Being ejected thence on account of his Independency, he taught classes till 1686,—Daniel De Foe being one of his pupils,—when he came to New England, eminent for learning and piety, as is evidenced by the report that he was invited to assume the presidency of Harvard College, which, it is said, was made up for by a pulpit in Charlestown.

The earliest record in England is 1655. The earliest here is at Charlestown, in 1690, October 13th. The last date in England is 1659. The observance was often interrupted, or the record has been lost. Certainly the record has been lost, and it is fair to presume that, in those stormy days, the meetings were irregular. It was natural that the outcasts should flock together for mutual support, enlightenment, and counsel, and that the exiles should continue in the new country a fellowship which they had formed in the old. They must hold to one another, for they were defenceless. The Association was formed " for promoting the Gospel and our mutual assistance and furtherance in that great work." It was a kind of clerical club intended to encourage the ministers and foster a fraternal feeling, and there was therefore a mingling in it of professional seriousness and personal warmth. The meetings were held at first once in a month, in Charlestown every six weeks; and always on Monday, at such hour as was most convenient, sometimes at nine o'clock in the forenoon. The scanty English records mention the examination and confirmation and ordination of candidates for the ministry as among the duties of the body, an important office in England, where the Puritans were jealously watched, and in America where they were few, and had to be careful lest wolves got into the sheepfold. A scribe was necessary to keep the records and a Moderator to preside at the meetings. The latter was chosen every time for the next assemblage, and one of his duties was to propose a subject for discussion. Forty or fifty questions were submitted in course of time, mostly relating to ecclesiastical and pastoral affairs, of course, but often social and ethical. This is a specimen:

"Whether an examination by the members is incumbent on those who wish to partake of the Lord's Supper"; "The marriage of cousins-german." The subjects were such as interested the members, and changed according to the exigency of the place and period,—now the speculative, now the moral predominating. Whatever the theme announced, the aim was practical. On several occasions a committee was appointed to present a list of questions. At one time a paper was read by some gentleman, of his own choice, and made the ground for discussion or conversation. Then, for a season, there was no formal topic. To strengthen the bond of union and render the meetings profitable was the end kept steadily in view. Several lists of questions are given in the record. It is not worth while to copy them, as they reflect simply the spirit prevailing at the period of their preparation, and if any were given all should be. It is enough to note here that the men were wide-awake—no fossils, no fogies, no priests. The following titles prove that: "Spiritualism," "Buddhism," "Social Meetings," "The Broad Church," "Prayers of Episcopacy," "Progress of Romanism," "The Advantages of Episcopacy," "Science and Faith," "Intemperance," "The Politico-Moral Aspect of the John Brown Tragedy," "The Abuses of Fast-Day," "The Sunday-School," "The Afternoon Service," "The War," "Slavery," "The Higher Law," "Individualism," "The Demand of the Times on us" (1862), "The Æsthetic Element in Worship," "Do we Need a New Cultus?" "University Education," "The Vices to which Ministers are Exposed," "Divorce," "The Ideal Church."

The meetings were in the afternoons at various hours—3:30, 4, 5, 5:30, as seemed expedient. Sometimes the business was all done before tea; sometimes the more serious part was introduced later. The exercises were always opened with prayer. In my youth the evenings were devoted to essay or discussion; at present the evening is free, and the whole business is finished between four and six o'clock. The oldest member is chosen Moderator, and he serves as long as he will. In regard to licensing ministers, it was unanimously voted, in 1854: 1. That this Association annuls any former vote or usage by which it may have recognized simple certificates of theological study or church membership as sufficient conditions for admission to our pulpits and for our participation in the ordination of candidates for the ministry. 2. That, to guide the future action of this Association in admitting candidates to the ministry, we require a testimonial from a member, or a brother minister introducing each candidate, and such an examination as may satisfy the brethren of his Christian belief and feelings for the ministry. 3. That, in thus returning to its former practice, this Association requires each candidate to present his testimonials at a meeting preceding that at which they are to be acted on, and also to prepare a discourse on some subject assigned at a previous meeting. 4. That, in conducting an examination of a candidate for the ministry, we shall consider it indispensable that the candidate express unequivocally his belief in the supernatural origin and character of Christianity. And the scribe was, by vote, instructed to communicate the foregoing resolutions to the ministerial associations enumerated in the Unitarian Congregational Register, and to the professors of our theological school.

The boundaries of the Association were at first restricted to Boston and its immediate vicinity; ministers of Chelsea and Braintree, who wished to come in, being courteously reminded that they lived beyond the precincts. The provision was necessary, as the towns multiplied and enlarged room had to be economized. It was a simple matter of space. There were twenty-seven members in 1847, and they were never all present at the same time. But they might be. The attendance was very uncertain. Much depended on the weather, or other engagements or attractions, and on the interest excited in the subject to be considered. Now and then the assemblage was too small for any discussion. Then again the parlor would be full. But the feeling of fellowship was warm and eager.

Rev. Thomas Gray, of Jamaica Plain, for many years Moderator of the Association, and the first candidate who was examined and approved by vote, as appears in the record, March 12, 1792, died on June 1, 1847, aged seventy-five years. He is spoken of as "of a gentle and kindly spirit. Those who were not his admirers, were his friends. He had no enemies."

The venerable Dr. John Pierce died in October, 1849, seventy-six years old and a little more. He was a member of the Association for upwards of half a century, its Moderator for six years, and seldom absent from the meetings. He was known for his many Christian virtues, was an ardent and active friend of temperance, and a sincerely humble, devout man. His sick chamber was a sacred and joyous spot which it was a privilege to visit. One hundred and twenty clergymen, representing seven different denominations, came there, and had their trust and hope confirmed. From his chamber he sent a greeting to his brethren of the Association, which responded through a special committee consisting of Francis Parkman, Ezra S. Gannett, and Samuel K. Lothrop. They said most truly: "To the satisfactions of such an union, you, dear Sir, have ever eagerly contributed. By the frankness and cordiality of intercourse, alike with the elder and the younger, by your hearty 'love of the brethren,' by your knowledge and faithful memory preserving for us the history of the past and the recorded wisdom of the fathers, you have been to us at once a counsellor and a brother."

When it came Dr. Parkman's turn to die (on November 12, 1852), he was celebrated as "one who loved his calling and discharged all its duties with untiring devotedness. As a preacher he was practical and evangelical. As a pastor tender and affectionate. He was a man of active and useful charities, a friend to learning, a punctual member or energetic officer of many literary, philanthropic, and religious associations, as well as a true friend of the worthy poor. He 'loved the brethren.' He was 'given to hospitality'—distributing to the necessities of saints."

Dr. Young was characterized as "to his congregation, an eloquent, sound and acceptable preacher, and a friendly pastor. And his brethren in the ministry will long deplore his removal from the midst of them."

A tribute was paid to Frederick T. Gray, the devoted minister, whose zeal and success were so conspicuous in developing the religious nature of the young, and among the poor, and who was distinguished as an inculcator of the plain, moral lessons of the New Testament. In the intervals of his last suffering he sent messages of affection to his friends, mentioning the "brethren" in the same breath with the "poor," and with "children."

The following affectionate mention of Rev. Dr. Samuel Barrett is copied from the record of June, 1866: "His kindly presence, his true spirit of Christian fellowship, his benign interest in all that is good, will be missed by the brethren with whom he rarely failed to meet until the disabilities of sickness were laid upon him."

On the decease of Dr. Frothingham—April 4, 1870 —the Association rendered a meed of praise. Its scribe was instructed to write a letter to the family, from which the following is an extract: "His brethren remember with pride the distinction with which he illustrated his sacred calling; but they cherish with joy the memory of the playful wit, the generous communication, the high example of scholarly attainment, the spiritual ideal, by which he enriched our meetings, and added a peculiar grace to our fellowship; and they are still cheered by the encouragement of his ministerial fidelity, the inspiration of his rare culture, the sweetness and sunshine of his faith."

This was the circle in which the genius of Dr. Frothingham shone. He delighted in the freedom, the respect for individual opinion, the sympathy in religious feeling. Its intercourse refreshed and aroused him; offered room for his mind, and space for the movement of his affections. His best things were said there, in the suddenness of immediate suggestion. But that nothing spoken in conversation was allowed to go upon the records, words of penetrating wisdom and acute criticism might be quoted. As it is, they must remain in the memory of those who heard them.

As originally constituted, the Association was, of necessity, Calvinistic. But disintegration began early. Theology became softened by rapid degrees. Even before the Revolution, schism set in. The writings of Thomas Paine were widely read, and new thoughts were suggested. The leaven of scepticism worked in high places. One by one men became dissatisfied with the prevailing tenets, and lost interest in the ancient connections. Arminianism crept in; Anti-trinitarianism was not uncommon; Universalism was diffused among the people. The ease with which King's Chapel was carried over from Episcopalianism to Unitarianism showed the popular tendency. The rights of reason and conscience were powerfully presented. The natural instincts of the heart cried loudly for recognition. So that, long before the final controversy, the cleavage was manifest. In my father's day Unitarianism was mixed with Orthodoxy, as it is even yet in some degree. But at recent meetings of the Association I have heard sentiments advanced that would not have been listened to half a century or even twenty-five years ago. By its liberality of expression the Boston Association became a nursery of liberal thinking. The heart has led the understanding.

X.

THE END.

My mother died in the summer of 1864. It was on the night of July 4th. She had seemed as well as usual, had sat on the piazza of her country house at Burlington, Massachusetts, and watched the sunset; then she went trustingly to bed, and never woke again. Her disease was consumption. She went to Europe, for the first time, in the spring of 1860, spent eighteen months abroad in perfect enjoyment, doing laborious things—ascending Vesuvius, for instance, —and came home in the autumn of 1861. A cold taken in the early winter settled on the lungs; a winter in Madeira, in 1862–3, did not effect a cure; the malady deepened, and proved fatal a little more than a year after her return. She was, in some respects, a remarkable woman, illustrating the old saying that extremes meet. She was a wonder of practical goodness, a marvel of kindly commonsense; simple in her tastes, plain in her habits, serious in her views of life, devoted to the customary daily duties of existence, gentle, patient, kind as the kindest to those who needed kindness most;

a mother who would give her life to her children; a wife who was all in all to her husband. Her crowning grace was affection; her distinguishing virtue was humility, which was unaffected. She was an enemy to all untruthfulness and all sentimentality. She needed no apostolic assurance to be convinced that "no man should think of himself more highly than he ought to think. . . If a man think himself to be something when he is nothing, he deceiveth himself." She had no doubt of it, and to her it seemed that the number of such self-deceived people was very large. She abhorred pretence so heartily that she was inclined to suspect it where it did not actually exist, and the inconsiderate might sometimes accuse her of not doing full justice to the sincerity which an appearance of vanity concealed from sight, not being metaphysician enough to distinguish between faults of physical organization and faults of moral character.

Connected with her humility in the sight of heaven was independence of the opinions of people and a singular frankness in expressing it. Her courage was unflinching. She shrank from nothing. No pain daunted her, no suffering. Not that she was insensible to agony; on the contrary, she felt it keenly; but when she was convinced that the inevitable must be borne, she submitted without a murmur or a remonstrance; she even insisted on the performance of whatever was necessary, enduring sharp torture, if required, rather than avoid what was repugnant to her judgment. She was no philosopher of any description or degree, but an honest, unsophisticated woman who took no merit to herself for what she did or was, and who, mindful of her own shortcomings, was not too ready to glorify the merits of others. To literary knowledge or judgment she made no claim; appreciating accomplishments in others, she possessed none of any kind. She was not "a woman of soul," nor any lover of such, though her habit of speaking no ill of her neighbor prevented her from wronging those she did not understand. She lived happily, and more than contented in her own world, accepting without question the place which divine Providence had assigned to her, satisfied that others should have their places. Her faith was that of a child in the institutions she was born under. If she had misgivings, she modestly kept them to herself. An optimist she was not; as little was she a pessimist. She had not the presumption to be either, probably she did not know what those cabalistical words meant. She was a true-hearted woman, who took things as they were without useless speculation or protest, and did what she could to make the world about her what it should be, by being a charitable friend to the poor, a helper to the weak, a consoler to the afflicted, a merciful judge to the erring. She was intelligent rather than intellectual, a fit companion for a man of interior habits, whose daily commerce was with the objects of an ideal sphere.

Her practical judgment, which was extraordinary, balanced his speculative insight; her single-minded, straightforward vision, disregarding incidental considerations of policy or comfort, but penetrating to the heart of the subject, was happily contrasted with a mental allsidedness which disqualified him for going at once to the central point in question; her brave acceptance of results eked out the timidity which shrank from occupying an exposed position; her solid weight of character held to the ground one whose tendency was to float too much in the air. She was a very strong woman, in her way, and had her lot fallen in the present generation, which attaches so much importance to the full development of feminine genius, she might have been as remarkable for mental as for moral quality. Though serenely happy, she was seldom gay; her moods were even. If she did not soar, she did not sink, and was the better able to meet the disappointments that crush volatile natures. When expectation flies low, the bolt of calamity causes no fatal fall. In enthusiastic days such a disposition appears sober and quiet, but in times of discomfiture it is a consoler and fortifier. She was, indeed, a helper and a caretaker. If she did not accompany her husband in his excursions to the high table-lands of literature, she surrounded his life with domestic influences that made him happy. Her active qualities were so strong, so sure, so steadfast and constant, that while she was all herself, those qualities that she was deficient in were not missed. It may be that her limitations, like the glass circlet which steadies the flame of the lamp, made her real power intense and luminous.

As I look back through the mist of years and recall these dear forms, freed from the trammels of earth and transfigured by memory, a feeling of shame comes over me that I did not better appreciate them when living; a feeling of gratitude for all their devotion in the time of my youth. My best gifts I trace to them, both of mind and character. To my father I owe what I may have of idealism, of imaginativeness, of fondness for literature, of fastidiousness in regard to persons and books, my conservatism of sentiment, my freedom of intellectual movement; only the wave goes up the shore farther than it did a generation ago, and I have spoken in public what he meditated in his study, carrying out what he adumbrated. To my mother is due a simplicity of purpose, a directness of aim, an outspokenness of conviction, a frankness aud fearlessness of utterance that, when fully developed, seemed to her rash if not supercilious. So easily is malleable iron changed into steel, and the ploughshare turned into a sword! Her loss was a heavy blow to him; not a sorrow merely, but a severe nervous and constitutional shock that affected even his physical nature, impairing his power of resistance. It was like taking away the prop he leaned on for daily support. He was weaker and more helpless. The year after her death he underwent an operation on his eyes. This was unsuccessful, and resulted in the extinguishment of the little light he had. He became totally blind, so that he could not distinguish light from darkness. The disease was of the nature of glaucoma, and was incurable. In-doors he was dependent on a reader, the daughter of his old friend Joseph T. Buckingham, a lady to whom in her youth he had been very kind, who was fond of books, conversant with ideas, and devoted to him, glad to serve him in his library and to read to him whatever he desired—articles in reviews, essays, novels, poems, stories. She was invaluable to him. Eyes was she to the blind, and feet was she to the lame in the house. Out of the house his son walked with him, guiding his steps through the thoroughfares of the city, and describing the monuments as they passed. I remember standing with him before the statue of Hamilton, then just erected in Commonwealth Avenue, and trying to bring it before his mind. And I remember one day in our walk telling him of a lady I had met who reminded me of mother. Hereupon he went into rapturous reminiscences, as if his past was ever present with him. And I remember how on his last bed, sitting by his side and wishing to say a comforting word, I spoke of the blessed people who were waiting on the other side to welcome him, and at the mention of his wife his face lighted up, the tears rolled down his cheek, and the consciousness of immediate distress was lost in the blissful prospect of joining her who had gone before. 'He was delighted to see his friends, entertaining them as of old with his wit, never dwelling on his disabilities, never complaining or repining, and making them happier than they were before. If there was occasion to speak of himself it was in a frank spirit, dutiful, trusting, and cheerful. "I shall try to behave," he said, and endeavor was required for that. His hours of weakness were few, his hours of distrust none. When heavier reading became unwelcome he fell back on lighter, and when this became unacceptable, the translation of German hymns was a resource. These were printed afterwards in the second series of the "Metrical Pieces." The solemn pathos, the fervent aspiration, the tender, filial spirit touched his sentiment, while the poetic form charmed his love of melody. I can see him now, sitting in his arm-chair, committing to memory the lines as they were read, turning them over in his mind and reproducing them in English, in the same metre as the original, always preserving the tone and, as nearly as possible, the expressions of his model. So full, active, precise was his mind! So intellectual were his tastes! So devout were his feelings! Thus it continued as long as any mental effort was possible, then he took to his bed, where he did not linger long ere death brought release.

At his funeral, his friend Dr. Hedge, among other things, said this:

As a preacher, he could hardly be said to be popular. Excessive refinement, want of *rapport* with the common mind, precluded those homely applications of practical truth which take the multitude. Nor did he feel sufficient interest in doctrinal theology to satisfy those who craved systematic instruction in that line. His reputation, therefore, was less extended than intense. The circle of his admirers was small; but those who composed it listened to him with enthusiastic delight. When, occasionally, he preached to us students at the University, from the pulpit of the College Chapel, there was no one, I think, to whom we listened with attention more profound; and, for myself, I can say with richer intellectual profit. The poetic beauty of his thought, the pointed aptness of his illustrations, the truth and sweetness of the sentiment, the singular and sometimes quaint selectness, with nothing inflated or declamatory in it, of the language, won my heart, and made him my favorite among the preachers of that day. I will not mispraise him when dead, whom living I could not flatter. I am well aware, and was even then aware, that the preaching of our friend did not satisfy the class of minds to which Channing in his way, and Walker and Ware and Lowell, so ably ministered in theirs; but preaching has other legitimate and important functions beside those of unfolding the philosophy of religion, or stimulating the moral sense. There are "differences of gifts," and there are "diversities of operations"; but the same spirit goes with all earnest effort in the service of truth, and is justified in all.

One service Dr. Frothingham has rendered to the Church and the cause of religion, in which he is unsurpassed by any preacher of his connection,—perhaps, I may say, by any American preacher of his time. I speak of his hymns, which will live, I believe,—I am sure they deserve to live,—as long as any hymns in our collections. His musical tact, his intimate knowledge of the exigencies of vocalism, combining with his poetic faculty, have added, in those hymns of his, to devout aspiration and pure religious sentiment the perfection of melody.

An exquisite finish, a polished elegance of thought and phrase, distinguished his performances, even the most trifling, and made them a study of good taste and good speech. In familiar discourse, when most at his ease, the unstudied and innate grace of his mind gave a peculiar and emphatic zest to his conversation. Nothing awkward ever fell from his lips. His words expressed with unerring fitness the thing most fit to be expressed. . . .

We love to remember, and shall long remember, the charm of his discourse, his wide culture, the sparkle of his wit, the flowers of rhetoric and song with which he adorned his path and gladdened ours. . . .

This was a man beloved of many, and most worthy to be loved, for his own sake, and the beautiful and endearing qualities which nearer acquaintance revealed in him. But love, it is said, is partial; it has no authorized voice in the court which tries character, either as witness or as judge. Love partial? I think not. Love can be critical; it is naturally so from its very concern for the good of its object. We see very clearly the faults of those we love, and we love them none the less on account of those faults. But then there are faults, and those of the worst kind, which preclude love; which alienate friendship, repel affection. Inordinate selfishness, vanity, falsity, malignity, arrogance, baseness of every sort,—these are qualities which no man can love. These are qualities no friendship can abide, which none can possess and continue to be loved. The fact, then, that he of whom I speak was so endeared to a large circle of attached friends, independently of all ties of kindred and blood,—friends whose friendship strengthened with acquaintance; who cleaved to him when all charm had vanished from his converse and all brilliancy had gone out of his life,—is a proof of the absence in him of all such qualities as I have named. But to speak positively of that which I found in him, I have to say that our friend, as I judged him, was truthful and sincere; gentle, generous, and kindly affectioned; humane, free from all arrogance or self-conceit; that his was the charity that "envieth not," that "vaunteth not itself," that "is not puffed up," that "thinketh no evil."

What especially impressed me in my long and close observation of the man, and what I consider to be a decisive test of character, was his prompt and generous recognition of talent, faculty, or merit in others; particularly in those of his own profession, competitors with him in a common career; the absence of any thing approaching to jealousy or bitterness, when the prize of popularity, denied to him, was freely bestowed on his inferiors. His eye was quick to discern, and his heart was prompt to appreciate, and his tongue to acknowledge, what was excellent in every performance, or the promise of excellence yet to come. He welcomed the rising talent of his juniors in office; he was even willing to believe in it where there was none. I am indebted to him for the best encouragement I received in my youth. Meanwhile, he never quarrelled with the want of appreciation of his own deserts; I think he underrated those deserts in his judgment of himself. He whom I was ready to place first was quite content to take the lower room.

Very little there was in him of wrath or ill-will, and that little very transient. At a time when the lines of ecclesiastical separation and sectarian exclusion were more distinctly and unrelentingly drawn than now, he could put himself in friendly relations with the ministers of other connections than his own. And if, in times of bitter controversy within the lines of his own denomination, he sometimes misjudged and burned with indignation against those whom he believed to be enemies of truth and religion,—enemies dangerous to social order,—in cooler moments he regretted with sorrow unfeigned every harsh and hasty word or act, and the severing of old bonds, and alienation and strife; and desired, as he assured me, to forget all differences, to recover past fellowship, and to be at peace with all the world.

The crowning grace of his life was the brave and invincible patience with which he bore the multiplied infirmities of his declining years.

There befell him in those years the affliction which is justly reckoned among the greatest of physical calamities—the loss of sight. Loss of sight to a scholar with a well-stored library, the habit of whose life has been to rove among his books, and to turn at any moment to the passage needed for solace or refreshment ; for the verification of a fact, for the resolution of a doubt ; or help in the perplexity of thought, where the right word at the right moment may roll the burden of hours from the mind ! Loss of sight to a widowed man, bereft of the one companion who best could lend her guiding hand to his dark steps, and best supply the lack of eyes at all times and in every place ! Loss of sight to a sensitive man, accustomed to self-help, and nobly impatient of foreign aid ! Loss of sight to a lover of nature, to whom the green of earth and the blue sky, and sunset and sunrise and the stars, are the heart's daily bread ! Friends, have you ever figured to yourselves what that means,—to be a prisoner with open doors ; a captive to your own impotence, walled in by perpetual darkness ; to know no difference between day and night ; to catch no eye responsive to your own, the light of no smile in the face of your beloved ; to miss forever the glories of earth and sky, the familiar aspects of every-day life, and all the dear consuetudes of vision ?

It was because Dr. Frothingham felt this that he consented to undergo an almost hopeless operation, —hopeless from the length of the disease and the excited condition of his mind. But, as he himself touchingly said : " Truly, the light is sweet, and a pleasant thing it is to behold the sun."

Rev. T. B. Fox, in the Boston *Evening Transcript* used the following language :

Quietly devoted to his professional duties, Dr. Frothingham's life was uneventful ; for it was the life of the student and the man of letters. His learning was various and accurate ; and he was honored for his acquirements, as well as for the high order of his intellectual gifts. In social converse he was the coveted teacher and companion of our best thinkers and scholars. His interest and delight in literary pursuits continued unabated when others, suffering from infirmities and pains like his, would have abandoned their books and pens, and felt that even to listen to reading was a luxury to be given up. Whilst sickness allowed him to work, he was never idle.

Dr. Frothingham published several volumes of prose and poetry ; and to the *Christian Examiner*, the *North American Review*, and several other periodicals, he frequently contributed articles of rare excellence, both as to their substance and their form. His style was singularly pure and rich ; showing a finish and correctness, in eloquent paragraphs and exquisite sentences, quite unrivalled. His exaction and fastidiousness, as a critic of the writings of others, were severely applied to his own productions ; and hence the polish, erudition, solid brilliancy, lofty sentiment and thoughtfulness, which have put them among the best specimens of American literature.

Of Dr. Frothingham as a man it is hardly necessary to speak in this community, to those of his own day and generation, or to those younger than himself, whose privilege it was to meet him and enjoy intercourse with him. Courteous, genial, hospitable, liberal in his conservatism, catholic in his judgments, free from all petty envies and jealousies, without ostentation, and scorning loud or mere professions, there was about him a winning charm that made his presence and his speech ever welcome to all.

It is impossible, in these necessarily hurried lines, to pay the tribute due to his home virtues, conscientious patriotism, assiduity as a Christian teacher, and readiness to contribute all in his power to the advancement of sound learning, wise charities, refining art, and whatever else might serve to promote the intellectual and moral well-being of the community.

To his excellence and his example in these respects others will hasten to do justice. We must be content with this general and imperfect expression of regard for the memory of one, whose works and words are not to be forgotten or the less prized, because the close of his more than threescore and ten years was veiled and hidden by blindness and inexorable disease.

Another friend and classmate bore witness to Dr. Frothingham's goodness of heart in these words:

I have personal knowledge of his kindness and generosity, for I have been the almoner of his bounty; and I know that some—I believe that many—recall his acts of kindness, and bless his memory.

With Dr. Frothingham died virtually his type of Unitarianism. It was the old-fashioned faith with a sentimental modification. The soul of a cast-off religion was in it; no new principle was adopted; no fresh law was invoked. Neither Channing's idea of the dignity of human nature, nor Mr. Parker's of another source of revelation, was accepted. It was "Christian" after the common definition, enlarged according to the enlightenment of the generation and the intellectual culture demanded of educated men. All speculative questions were avoided. The preaching was almost entirely practical, and practical after the ancient pattern, not according to modern ideas, humanitarian and social. Penitence was inculcated and humiliation, and veneration, and almsgiving, and self-distrust, and thankfulness for usual mercies, and dependence on divine Providence, and submission of reason to revelation. Even men like James Walker and John Gorham Palfrey dwelt much on the virtues of "piety" so called. Alexander Young was a good example of the usage popular at that time among "liberal Christians," moving, as they did, along the sober level of the common morality, un-ecclesiastical, undogmatical, following the line of simple, plain, average duty. My father tried to render this poetical and in a sense ideal; but it seldom or never rose to the height of the spiritual. Unitarianism could not be called dry or negative, while its ethics were so vital, but it certainly was not succulent or deeply interior. It was a reasonable, becoming, dignified, respectable, elegant in its best aspect, delicate system, not severely naturalistic, and only gently scholarly; conservative, of course, as well of religious as of social traditions, it was in no condition to sustain a shock from either quarter. It was natural that educated, cultivated people of literary tastes and high social position, self-respecting, stable, gentlemanly, should connect themselves with Unitarian societies, for such were supported by external props, and the congregations were, in fact, composed of the comfortable, the well-to-do, the respectable. Efforts were made to prove that Unitarianism was adapted to the poor, the untaught, the simple, the tempted, the miserable, but these attempts were never conspicuously successful. The majority of men preferred Calvinism with its mysticism and its fervor. Natural conscience was not enough for them, nor were their minds sufficiently strong to grasp conceptions purely rational. Ernest Renan's criticism in his article on "Channing and the Unitarian Movement in the United States," in the "Études d'Histoire Religieuse" is substantially just, though more true of Unitarianism than of Dr. Channing. He describes it as "une theologie a la Franklin sans grande portée metaphysique ni visée transcendentale." "On ne refait pas un rêve par un acte de la volonté." He compares St. Francis d'Assisi with Channing, and while admitting the intellectual absurdity of the old religions, contends for their power over the imagination. This, Unitarianism, however reasonable, never had, neither had it the exaltation of sentiment which, however far from being sensible, was captivating to the soul. The denial of the most irrational yet most fascinating and impressive doctrines—the depravity of human nature, atonement, election, substitution, everlasting punishment—was precisely the cause of its rejection by the mass of mankind; more especially as no equally absorbing ideas were substituted for them. This gave the dry, cold, barren, negative character the system clearly had in the popular judgment. It was in vain to appeal to texts of Scripture. The Bible was not to the multitude a text, but the whole mind of God; a mystery, to be interpreted by the soul, not by the understanding. The creed, also, was inspired in the common apprehension, and, being the later version of the divine thought, could rightfully explain the earlier revelation; so that nothing was gained by so-called clearness or simplicity of statement. The very notion of inspiration implied a fulness of meaning that the human intellect could not measure; the most obscure hints might contain the deepest intimations of superhuman intelligence; and even when nothing was spoken to the outward ear the inward ear might be audibly addressed. This was a weak point of the Unitarianism we are considering. If it could have discarded entirely the belief in the inspiration of Scripture and planted itself squarely upon the spiritual laws as disclosed to the soul, as Emerson did, its path would have been plain. But this was impossible; half-way measures were all that presented themselves, and these did not cripple its march. It appealed to nature and yet accepted the supernatural. It denied the deity of Christ and still called him the Son of God. It ascribed moral attributes to persons, but termed him Saviour, Redeemer, Mediator, lavishing on him every epithet of glory. It received the stories of the resurrection, the ascension, the raising of the dead, the multiplication of the loaves, miracles, prophecies, and yet applied reason to the story of the superhuman birth. The truth is that it did not carry out any fundamental principles of doubt. The criticism was neither brave nor thorough. In theology there was no criterion but common-sense. In the matter of the Scriptures, the old tradition was substantially adhered to. The inspiration of the Bible was taken for granted. Prophecy was trusted in. Superhuman influence was claimed, and although a spiritual meaning was inserted when the letter was revolting or absurd, the divine mind was supposed to be at work. The conclusions of Andrews Norton, an accomplished and elegant scholar, severe after his way in his strictures on the "sacred text," were tacitly received as final. He was the great authority, as bold, fearless, truthful as he was exact and careful. What he discarded as ungenuine might safely be thrown aside; what he admitted as part of the original writing could be safely relied on. Most of these Unitarians pinned their faith unreservedly to him, and were satisfied with his argument for the genuineness of the Gospels. The few who were not, fell back on the books themselves as being of providential and therefore unaccountable origin. A good example of these latter is furnished by the following extract from a letter of my father to Mr. Norton in regard to his demonstration of the authorship of the four Gospels.

"My notion of the matter is that no hypothesis explains the composition and mode of growth of those wonderful books. Remarkable in every thing else, they are remarkable also in being without father or mother, as Melchisedec was before them. Like the Nile to the ancients, they hid their source. It does appear to me impossible, on the face of the record, that such writings should be independent writings, and I can come to no theory that shall explain to me how they arose. Well, then, I can do without any theory, and acknowledge my ignorance. . . . It does not seem to me that the supposition of genuineness accounts for the phenomena; and therefore your theory fails to satisfy me, as much as the minute inventions of the 'common-document' men, and the 'copying-of-one-another' men. This being my view of the subject, you see what a wide field of skirmish I have chosen for myself. No heavy-armed soldier or close-combatant am I."

This candid evasion of the difficulty escapes from the point of the sword, but leaves the way open to sentiment and to any amount of faith. The weeding out of the tares had no effect in impairing the sanctity of the record. The approach of the scalpel was not dreaded. Thus, whether Mr. Norton's hypothesis was welcomed or not, inspiration was preserved; for Mr. Norton, too, was a reverent believer, and having, as he felt sure, clarified the Word, he gave himself up without reserve to the motives of a tender and trustful heart. Criticism, in his hands, was any thing but cold. Not many did as much as he to promote evangelical feelings among his fellow-believers. He was a man of the warmest affections, as was shown in his ardent friendship for Charles Eliot, and in his childlike piety. This union of loyalty to the truth and personal devotion explains the serenity of faith which the Unitarians cherished. Criticism, as we know it, had not reached here so early; in fact much of it was unborn. Ewald's "History of Christ and His Age" was not published till 1857, twenty years after the letter to Mr. Norton, quoted above, was written. Kuenen was unheard of, and even if his studies had been familiar, they would have been remanded to the category of theories, while piety would have continued to regard the Bible as the word of God. Since Ferdinand Christian Baur could preach in a Lutheran pulpit and at the same time, in his lecture-room, teach that the Gospels were literary pamphlets, *tendenz-schriften*, it is not surprising that earlier disciples paid no heed to a criticism which was far less destructive. It is the evil of divorcing knowledge from faith that justice is done to neither. Knowledge is discredited, is consigned to a subordinate, not to say an insignificant position; and faith is degraded from a spiritual principle to a sentimental feeling, based upon tradition. Knowledge was simply held at arm's length instead of being invited to take full possession of its own department and extend the literary laws over their whole legitimate domain. Criticism, it is true, had not gone far at that time, but it had gone far enough to establish its method and to show the distinction between the two provinces of faith and reason.

The unconsciousness of any radical change in religious ideas is revealed in a hymn which my father wrote for me, in December, 1863. It was not suspected that the authority of Scripture would be rejected, that the story of Jesus would be discredited, that the Christ of the Church and the Creed would be repudiated, that the Fatherhood of God would be called in question, and that the fundamental doctrines of theism would be doubted, by religious men too, and in the name of a spiritual faith. This hymn was one of the last he wrote.

ON THE DEDICATION OF THE HOUSE OF WORSHIP OF THE THIRD UNITARIAN SOCIETY, NEW YORK, DECEMBER 25, 1863.

One Father, God, we own ;
 One Spirit evermore ;
One Christ, with manger, cross, and throne,
 The Light, the Way, the Door.

In souls we hail his birth ;
 'T is now he comes again :
His kingdom is the convert earth,
 His Church all faithful men.

The Scriptures thus we read ;
 Of strangest powers compiled,
To mould the heart, and clear the creed
 Of earth's frail, clouded child.

Its essence, not its writ,
 Our sovereign rule we call ;
Not fastening down all truth to it,
 But widening it to all.

With this free reverence, Lord,
 In Christly church estate,
With earnest, brotherly accord,
 These walls we dedicate,

To prayer and holy thought ;
 Affections set above ;
To faiths from highest fountains brought,
 And works of widest love.

Thy presence, Father, make
 The refuge and supply ;
And for thy Truth and Mercy's sake
 Build on, and sanctify.

The scientific question had not fairly come up. True, the utmost liberality towards it was expressed, but its array was visible only very far off, on the outskirts of the Old Testament, in a discussion of a problem in Genesis. At this distance, science could hardly awaken alarm; nor was it difficult to speak brave words in an article on "Man before Adam." But how would the doctrine of evolution have been met, reversing as it does the entire order of creation, reconstructing the history of the Bible, and making necessary a fresh definition of Providence? Spencer's doctrine would simply have been classified as one of the guesses, and Darwin's theory would have been unanswered. The least touch on the vitals of religion, as it was then considered, would have been resented, and the arms would still have clung to the Cross. Few even yet have the courage to follow out the implications of evolution to their last consequences. Fifty years ago nothing threatened the foundations of belief or laid violent hands on the outer walls of revelation, nor was it surmised that the danger might come nearer. If it had been, the old assumptions would have been retained, and the foe, instead of being faced in the fight, or even fought behind battlements, would have been scornfully waived off as not fit to encounter the hosts of the revealed God. Half a century ago the prepossessions covered a great deal of ground. Now the ground is disputed inch by inch, but it *is* disputed. Then it was not so much as disputed, for the adversary was never confronted. Joseph Priestley, whose fame as a scientific man extended over Europe, and who suffered for heresy, held to biblical infallibility as long as he lived, his island being guaranteed against the most formidable seas. Theodore Parker defended, and must have defended to the last, his view of theism; and James Martineau contends passionately against the materialists. The Boston Unitarians followed in the footsteps of Priestley. The scientific spirit is of recent origin. It certainly does not ask that any genuine conviction shall be surrendered, for it wants a struggle in order that its own beliefs may be certified; but it does require that whatever convictions are entertained shall be held in accordance with the method of science. It will have no arbitrary reserves, no unassailable positions. But no such refuge as agnosticism, no cloudy screen, was necessary in the last generation. Faith asked no apology. The tradition was secure, so that ignorance was justified in asserting the tradition. I was present at the Berry Street Conference when Theodore Parker flung into the teeth of a doctor of divinity the miracle of the loaves, and when the latter declined being catechised, on the ground of ill-health! And, on another occasion, Mr. Parker asked a prominent divine if Jesus exhausted the infinite. "Pretty much," was the reply.

That Unitarianism should have no science is then not surprising. That it should have no decisive philosophy, is; for the system was founded upon a philosophy, such as it was. Transcendentalism had a bad name, as being associated with German thought, destructive criticism, unbelief, radicalism of all sorts, and as rendering useless the reliance on miracle, prophecy, and external revelation ;—though the belief in man's spiritual nature involved its cardinal axioms. Sensationalism was repudiated, because it seemed to limit mind and conscience, though it legitimated its favorite credences. As a rule, the Unitarians were "sensationalists," so far as they were any thing, though this was held in too crude a form to satisfy all, so nothing was professed. To illustrate: when I was in my first pastorate, I became a transcendentalist, and as such made light of the outward props on which the people had been taught to depend. We fell into collision therefore, almost without knowing why. In one of my frequent notes to my father I expressed my discontent and put my finger on the cause,—my transcendentalism and their sensationalism. My father evidently did not appreciate the antagonism of the two systems. Why trouble yourself, he said, about such a distinction? They know nothing of it, and you need say nothing. Go on as if it did not exist, and confine yourself to undisputed points. As if there were any! Channing—though his faith had not worked itself clear, and he still had hanging round his mind the rags of the old theology—had nevertheless a positive intellectual faith; a faith in the immanence of God in man. Theodore Parker distinctly abandoned the sensational philosophy, preached the sonship of the soul, and allowed free course to biblical criticism, discrediting every principle that appealed to external authority. His transcendentalism it was, in fact, that made him so willing to accept the results of "German rationalism." But convictions such as his led at once to social radicalism, the bugbear of Unitarianism. Channing took an interest in temperance, in prison reform, in education, in the future of the working man, in the slave; attended the Chardon Street Conference, encouraged experiments like that of Brook Farm, cautiously but deeply meditated fundamental social changes. Parker was an earnest reformer in many directions. So was Emerson. Ripley, a purely intellectual man, called himself by every name that was offensive to polite ears. There was not a transcendentalist who was not, in some measure, an anti-slavery man, and thus a reproach. The Unitarians were conservative, believers in providential arrangements of society, believers in respectability, in class distinctions. They did not, by any means, want to keep things as they were, but they did not want any sudden overturning, or any *overturning* at all. Their faith was in slow and gradual uplifting, through the diffusion of charity and the spread of truth. Their philosophy lent itself most readily to this; therefore they were sensationalists, rather from social feeling than from metaphysical thinking. I am afraid, too, they avoided close analysis of ideas, as committing them to a theory the results of which might cramp the movement of their minds, or compromise their position in the community. They, more naturally, clung to tradition, and stood where the divine will had placed them. As Puritans, they believed in the unadulterated influence of the Christian religion, in the Scriptures, in the Christ, in the sacraments of the Church. The theological account of all this was partially discarded; some of it was absolutely repudiated—all that offended the moral sense; some was merely attenuated—the doctrine of inspiration, for instance, the rank of Jesus, the virtue of the bread and wine of the supper. With purely philosophical problems they did not much concern themselves. This was a matter of speculation, not of practice, and their business was to edify; and if any were interested in such curious speculations as those respecting the origin of ideas, they might follow them up, as scholars, in the study. These things must always remain in dispute; meanwhile moral impressions were certain, and it was a great deal wiser to hold by what was approved.

In spite of their want of science; in spite of their indifference to philosophy; in spite of the vagueness of their theological opinions, these men were real friends of intellectual freedom, genuine promoters of mental independence. The hazy character of their theology, the æsthetic rather than dogmatic tone of their creed, aided this tendency by leaving their minds at liberty to cultivate literature. The insensibly secular cast of their thought opened the world of poetry and domesticated the best classics among them. Unconsciously they were Greek and not Asiatic, Western, not Oriental in their culture. Their libraries were miscellaneous, not so much theological as literary in the human sense. The world's books were on the shelves, the masterpieces of Athenian, Roman, English, French, German wisdom; poetic, dramatic, epic, heroic. Unitarianism has always been accompanied by this love of gentile lore. Said a lady to Edward Everett Hale :

A Unitarian church to you merely means one more name on your calendar. To the people in this town it means better books, better music, better sewerage, better health, better life, less drunkenness, more purity, and better government.

" Well," said the Boston *Herald*, " this is the whole issue in a nutshell." This implied a free range of intelligence, confidence in the rational uses of mind, a broad conception of truth, emancipation from doctrinal trammels. While such productions were not received as, in any way, a substitute for Holy Scripture, or even as a rival to the word of revelation, it was a good deal to countenance them, and give them a place in human culture. Puritanism began this encouragement of intellect when it founded Harvard College ; and though it supposed that the effect would be evangelical, still it opened the door wide to the spirit of undogmatic liberty, and led directly to the idea of ethnic scriptures which distinguished the *Dial*. I remember reading in my youth, to my father's entire satisfaction, the works of Æschylus and Plato, nor was the least suggestion made that something else might be more edifying. The notion of culture was already supplanting that of conversion, and width of view was coming to take the place of "the one thing needful." No objection was made to our reading novels on Sunday. Such books were, of course, regarded as recreations merely, and were never supposed to nourish the "soul," but it was something to allow that they could do so much, and were not wholly abominable. The barrier between "sacred" and "profane" compositions existed, but it was not so high that it could not be jumped over. Soon it was to be removed entirely. In the meantime Unitarianism was preparing the way for this final consummation. Unless my memory deceives me, the beginnings of a decided intellectual deliverance from the bondage of tradition can be traced back to my boyhood. I say the beginnings; the full development came later. When reason was first liberated, none but its enemies foresaw its ultimate triumph. The sole effectual method of dealing with it was to put it under the ban, with all its works, and keep it firmly under lock and key, with a perpetual guard to stop its escape. As soon as Protestantism, in the innocence of its heart set it free, with its wonted proclivity to take an ell where an inch was granted, it put forth its claims. The struggle against creed and Church was long and desperate, as both had power, wealth, and prescription on their side; until now the fury of the battle, at least with thinking people, is about over. The calmness of assured triumph is not attained except by the few, whose weapons of war are in their sheaths; to the multitude, reason is still an enemy whose attacks are to be feared, but who is certain to be conquered at last. During the long course of its effort to gain headway against ecclesiasticism and dogmatism, reason contracted an aggressive, self-asserting, defiant character that ages only will overcome. Hitherto it has been destructive, but it will not be so always. By and by it will be constructive, and will work to establish belief on rational grounds. This is all it asks for,—an opportunity to display its full power as an organizing faculty, a force of thought taking the place of tradition. What surprises us in the old Unitarianism is the sweetness of its quality, its geniality, its hospitable, buoyant spirit. Several causes aided this: its undogmatic attitude; its freedom from contention; its indifference to sectarian distinctions; its unconsciousness of any break or absolute departure from the ancient credence, which it modified but did not abolish; its quiet assurance of faith; its abstention from social polemics, sure to run at last into the bitterness of opposition; its undisturbed possession of the literary field in its most innocent aspect of classical prose and poetry; its confinement to the realm of taste for beauty in style, and the presentation of good thoughts in lofty and pure form; its preference of sentiment to ratiocination. Channing's sweetness was in a great measure due, I always thought, to the invalidism that kept him secluded from popular strife; Parker's to his natural disposition, inherited from his mother, and fortified by training. But the sweetness of the regular Unitarians belonged to their neutral position as a conservative body of men who took no part in any disputes, whether doctrinal or social, who believed dutifully, and who studied faithfully as their inclination prompted. It must not be inferred that there was no religiousness among the Unitarians. There was a good deal. It was not characteristic of the body. In many cases it was a sentiment rather than a principle, a prompting of duty rather than an impulse of feeling. It is difficult to combine spirituality with the critical understanding. But the little book, by Henry Ware, Jr., on the "Formation of the Christian Character," was to the Unitarians what Thomas à Kempis' "Imitatio" was to the Catholics, or Law's "Serious Call" was to the Orthodox Protestants.

A very admirable trait in Unitarianism was its reverence for personal character. It was balanced, even, moderate. Its friends were not ascetic in any sense or in any degree. They lived as generously as was comely, after the manner of their time, which was plain, simple, undemonstrative, restrained. They were not vegetarians, they were not total abstainers, they did not wear hair shirts, or live in hovels, or severely mortify the flesh. But they were never excessive in their use of the good things of this world. They were temperate *in all things,* ever keeping conscience and good-sense uppermost, leading a reasonable, sober, dignified existence, all the higher in tone for the modest indulgences they permitted to themselves, but kept in check.

On the restoration of the Federal Street theatre to its originally destined use in 1846, my father wrote some lines, which were printed but not offered for recitation or prize, probably because such performance was thought to be inconsistent with the clerical profession. But a delight in the theatrical art belonged to him, and he never visited New York without going to see William Burton, and getting the creases of professional care taken out of him by that laughter-provoking comedian.

Not the ministers only, but the laity had this virtuous, grave, healthy moral character, genial, but upright, honest, and chaste. A singular purity marked all their behavior. Integrity was their distinction from highest to lowest. Their enemies admitted as much when they reproached them for being simply moral men ; as if character was not the consummate flower of faith ; as if goodness such as theirs would not sweeten the world ; as if a practical allegiance to the cardinal ideas of religion—God, immortality, the divine origin of truth—was a sign of decay and not of growth ; as if the decline of theological animosity was not an absolute gain, and the postponement of creed to conduct was not a thing to be welcome ! Indeed, the best that can be said of this much-abused Unitarianism is this respect for worth. If any fault may be found with it, it must be on the score of its rigidity. It was a little too unbending in its judgments, a little too abrupt. There was some want of shading. If conduct was not right it was wrong. White existed, black existed; but gray did not exist. Yet, in these days of allowance, of charity, of all-sidedness, of studied fairness, such ethical dogmatism is somewhat refreshing. True, it betrayed a lack of color, but this is cancelled by the single-minded integrity that walked straight and clean through the crooked and dirty places of life. This uprightness might, in part, have been due to a certain narrowness of perception imposed by social usages, that were not elastic as they are now; but even this may be pardoned on account of the virtue which is so precious. Breadth is an excellent quality, but it is dearly purchased at the expense of sturdiness of will. It must be a high type of humanity that can keep pace with the utmost liberalism, matching its mental largeness with a corresponding moral courage. Boston was a little city; everybody was known; everybody had a reputation to maintain; the stays of society were against all walls to shore them up. Now the town is much larger and more under mercantile influences; and it is mainly by falling back on old reliances that the ancient standard of character can be preserved. One is somehow obliged to contract his world if he would prop up his morale, and the Unitarians were fortunate in being able to live in their little universe and yet maintain their souls alive. Modern Unitarianism is a very different system, more social, more ethical, more reformatory, more scientific, more democratic, more willing to accept the results of radical criticism, more rationalistic, more philosophical, but its firmness of texture is largely owing to the training it derived from its ancestors, and the noble examples of the fathers who preceded them in establishing the supremacy of the attributes on which society reposes. However broad the faith may be, however indifferent to theological definitions, however elastic in sympathy, however enthusiastic for progress, it will always be mindful of its origin; it will always be grateful to its creators; it will always set character before credence; and, being confident of its principles, will allow free movement to the mind.

In this brief sketch description has been purposely avoided of several important men, who were either well enough known already from being written about, or who have made a single impression, or who have been distinguished in other fields,—men like Charles Lowell, John Thornton Kirkland, Joseph McKean, Thaddeus Mason Harris, John Pierce, Jos. Allen, Thomas Gray, the Wares—Henry, Henry Jr., William,—Samuel Gilman, Wm. H. Furness, Alvan Lamson, Ephraim Peabody, James Walker, John G. Palfrey, Edward B. Hall, George Putnam, Francis W. P. Greenwood, Ezra Stiles Gannett, Robert C. Waterston, Frederick H. Hedge, R. W. Emerson,

John H. Morison, Henry W. Bellows, Cyrus A. Bartol, George E. Ellis, William Newell, William B. O. Peabody, Oliver W. B. Peabody, Andrew P. Peabody, Andrews Norton. These were all remarkable men, many of them very remarkable, in different ways, as preachers, theologians, philosophers, writers, ministers, critics, philanthropists, poets,—men of unusually large cultivation, even of saintly disposition; men of decided individuality; men, oftentimes, of genius, brilliant, profound; men of mind and of soul. On reading their works two things have struck me: first, their moderation of view, their freedom from partisanship, their reluctance to commit themselves to systems of thought, their devotion to the practical aspects of opinion. They kept their critical and philosophical speculations, so long as they were mere speculations—useless for edification, —to themselves or the seclusion of the study; saying nothing about them in public, exercising, in fact, a continence that was misunderstood, being construed as timidity or hypocrisy, when, in truth, it was merely a persuasion on their part that surmises of this kind were unfruitful in their influence on the religious life. This was the one interest to be regarded by the clergyman, and was to be watched over strictly. Questions of theology were of small moment when the spiritual welfare was concerned. They confined themselves, therefore, to the work of increasing the sum of moral sentiment. In the second place, I have been impressed with the prominence given to the literary as opposed to the controversial temper. Most of these men preferred to write essays, narratives, poems, biographies; to pursue studies in history, science, botany; to read Goethe, Schiller, Molière, Shakespeare; to cultivate art, music, the drama. An atmosphere of elegant taste pervades the denomination. Even when occasion calls for polemics the argument is usually conducted after the manner of one more interested in the style than in the dogmas under discussion, and who would be gladly let off from the duty of debate. In A. P. Putnam's volume, "Singers and Songs of the Liberal Faith," there are more than seventy names, and these are but a portion of the versifiers. The larger number are clergymen, but there are upwards of a score of laymen and more than a dozen women. It is true that the wealth of our poetry is not much increased by this contribution, but it indicates the bent of the denomination, and it shows how, in this estimation, all the religious sentiments naturally ran to music.

There has been, in all ages, an indifference to theology, as the theory, the doctrinal account of religion. The Catholic mystics felt it; the Protestant mystics felt it; the devout, the spiritually minded, the seraphic of every communion, Quakers, Unitarians, disciples of the inner light, have felt it. But this kind of indifference was occasional, not general, not native to the sect. There was no systematic repudiation of the validity of a doctrinal scheme. The belief was accepted and was merely abandoned in times of exaltation. The Unitarians were the first, so far as I know, who deliberately substituted a rational idealism for the creed; who adopted art, humanity, literature as expressions of the divine mind; who set up social morality as a means of grace. Spirituality was not conspicuous among them, in the usual acceptation of the term. Even Emerson, their chief idealist, beamed with a mild radiance, spoke wisely of the spiritual laws, and was supremely interested in ethical principles. There were theologians among them; there were disputants; but as an order there was very little concern with doctrinal distinction. They were scholars, pastors, readers of books. Secular culture came up in their generation. Dogmatism received its death-blow. The creed was forgotten. The subsequent detachment from the theological method in favor of the scientific, which has been gaining ground during the last thirty years and has reached its culmination now, is, in my judgment, largely due to the example of these men.

Nor is it surprising that they kept theology, though in the background, and were ready to fall back on it whenever they felt called to bring forward the reasons for their faith. The era of a purely spiritual belief had not fairly come. It was a solitary, personal thing, peculiar to a few men, who stood by themselves. Most wanted a tradition, a system that had roots, that was held by generations of men, that had its saints and martyrs, that could appeal to its sanctities, could bring learning and attested piety to its support, and was recommended by experience. Though in details it may have been modified, some parts being dropped and others altered, the substance of it remained the same, and they knew no other guarantee. That of the soul they could not comprehend, for the soul shared the infirmity of human nature, which, in their opinion, needed regeneration. The idea of an incorruptible humanity was still far from them, and they clung to some external revelation which was susceptible of demonstration. They entertained no oracles except the "oracles of God." They did not think it necessary to call attention to their tenets any more than to their cellars, which nevertheless existed, as all men were aware, and could be shown on occasion. Generally they might be taken on trust. A stranger taking up his residence in the city, and asking about Unitarian churches, was recommended to go to Dr. Frothingham's, for there he would hear less about "Christ" than elsewhere. This was not because Dr. Frothingham believed so little, but because he believed so much. He had no faith "to speak of"; it could bear silence.

Neither had the gospel of individualism become familiar, as it has been for the last forty years. During the transcendental period, individualism was preached as a duty, a sacred obligation imposed by the spiritual laws. Before this period was fully inaugurated and had settled down into systematic ways, it meant simply confusion and was repelled by lovers of order. When it had passed, individualism gave place to a reign of law which became a substitute for tradition, and authority was transferred from Scripture to philosophy, the new word of the Highest. The philosophy of Channing had disappeared. The philosophy of Parker would not bear analysis. The old theology would submit to no further attenuation. Transcendentalism had gone. Sentimentalism was out of date. A new gospel for Liberalism,—faith founded on knowledge and sustained by inquiry,—must be the spiritual religion of the future.

But this is not a development from Unitarianism, properly so-called; still less is it a continuance of Channing or Parker. For though the former always remained within the limits of the recognized faith, and first awakened the Unitarian controversy, and is regarded as the father of the sect, still he would never assume a party name, evidently feeling that he did not belong to a denomination, and he introduced a principle which, fairly carried out, as it was by Emerson, Ripley, Alcott, and the Transcendentalists generally—I allude to his doctrine of the essential worth of human nature—was irreconcilable with any form of evangelical belief, founded, as this was, upon the need of supernatural redemption by a disordered race; while the latter, though claiming to be a consistent Unitarian, substituted a new basis for religion which not merely dismissed the dogma of depravity, but rendered unnecessary a revelation or a saviour. The erection of another tribunal—the soul—made Scripture superfluous and dethroned Jesus.

It is true that Unitarianism was somewhat confused by the admixture of incongruous elements, beside the unavoidable imperfection of its exegesis. George Ripley reckoned my father among the early Transcendentalists, a classification in which the good man would not have taken supreme delight. James Walker and William P. Lunt used the intuitive philosophy, the one to legitimate faith, the other to furnish a ground for the religious emotions; but the main drift was certainly in the opposite direction. There was a vehement protest against such doctrines of Calvinism as an endless hell, the damnation of infants, the perdition of the heathen, but this was simply the outcry of the natural heart and conscience which had by this time emancipated themselves from dogma, and were not afraid to assert the claims of pity, mercy, kindness, common humanity. No philosophical ideas were involved in this assertion. The moral indignation at the horror of war or the enormities of slavery was simply human. It would have been strange indeed if cultivated men in the nineteenth century had been indifferent to evils that were thrust upon their notice. The wonder is that they were so much so as they were; they would have been far more outraged, if a deep-seated principle had impelled them.

The Unitarians appealed to the Bible, and went no further. They were shut up in its enclosure, and will always be. They identified religion with Christianity and Christianity with the Scriptures. Efforts will continue to be made to bring the New Testament into line with the latest spiritual experiences, but the ancient tradition will not, in their case, be transcended.

The new Unitarianism, as it is termed, is neither sentimental nor transcendental nor traditional. It is rather historical and experimental. It does not grow out of the old. It oversteps the boundary of Scripture and even of Christianity, and is a form of theism; theism generously interpreted in accordance with knowledge, thought, science, spirituality. It is a religion of aspiration, poetic feeling, imagination, prescience. Its doctrine about God is rational, scientific, human, answering the needs of the highest ideality. Its immortality is a hope, a trust, a consolation for sorrow, an incitement to endeavor, a faith of the human race, the last term of evolution, an inference from a spiritual nature in man, a necessary complement to destiny, an anticipation of future blessedness, a promise of full fruition,—never a traditionary belief. It conceives of moral law as an element inwrought into the nature of things, or a product of the best experience, or the feeling of exalted souls, or an attribute of the normal conscience —never as an echo from Sinai or a breath from the mountain of the Beatitudes. In a word, it is an elevated kind of religious faith, simple and devout. It calls itself Unitarian simply because that name suggests mental freedom, and breadth, and progress, and elasticity, and joy. Another name might do as well, perhaps be more accurately descriptive. But no other would be as impressive, or, on the whole, so honorable.

INDEX.

A

Abolitionists, 194, 197-199
Adams, Charles Francis, 94
Adams, Henry, 195, 196
Alcott, Bronson, 264
Allen, J. H., 210, 212
Allston, Washington, 6
Alps, the, 147
Ancestry, 15
Anthology Club, 19, 206
Antinomian Controversy, 30
Arnold, M., quoted, 91
Asceticism among the Unitarians, 256, 257
Ashburton, Lord, 122
Association, American Unitarian, 64
Association, Boston, of Congregational ministers, 33, 184, 213
Athenæum, 19

B

Bacon, Francis, 176
Bancroft, George, 139, 140, 160
Barnard, Charles, 65
Barrett, Samuel, 65, 160, 161, 225
Bartol, C. A., 58, 160, 216
Baur, F. C., 57, 246
Belgium, 145
Bellows, H. W., 210
Benevolent Fraternity of Churches, 65
Berne, 147
Berry Street Conference, 63
Bigelow, Jacob, 94
Blindness, 155, 238
Books, 18

Boston, 17, 20, 127
Bowditch, Dr. N., 94
Breakfasts in London, 141
Briggs, G. W., 190
Brooks, Ann Gorham, 93, 228, etc., 233
Brooks, Peter Chardon, 21, 93, 94 etc., 126, 203
Buckingham, Ellen, Miss, 233
Buckminster, J., quoted, 196
Buckminster, J. S., 23, 75

C

Carlyle, Thomas, 60, 142
Channing, W. E., 13, 27, 49, 101, 125, 139, 160, 161, 168, 193, 211, 251, 255, 264
Character among the Unitarians, 256
Charles X., 135
Chauncy, Charles, 28
Church, First, in Boston, 26, 33
Church, the Temple, in London, 141, 144
Clarke, James Freeman, 35, 61, 62, 190, 193
Cities, Peculiarities of, 140
Clergy, 23
Cotton, John, 20, 34
Cousin, Victor, 152
Covenant of First Church, 29

D

Dewey, Orville, 3, 69, 160, 211
Diman, J. L., 35
Disciple, Christian, the, 207
Doyle, J. A., 69, 201
Dwight, Theodore, quoted, 194

E

Eliot, Charles, 94
Elliot, Samuel, 102
Ellis, A. B., 36
Ellis, G. E., 160, 169, 210
Ellis, Rufus, 35, 154, 160, 193
Emerson, R. W., 10, 13, 26, 57, 60, 70, 101, 102, 126, 160, 168, 180, 243, 251, 262, 264
Everett, Edward, 23, 76, 94, 129, 141, 158, 160, 181, 194, 197, 201
Examiner, Christian, the, 60, 206–208

F

Felton, C. C., 159
Fields, J. T., 165
Follen, Charles, 49
Fourier, Charles, 142
Fox, T. B., 210, 238
Francis, Convers, 72, 160, 186 etc., 193
Freeman, James, 160
Frothingham, N. L., 11, 15, 16, 22, 24, 27, 52, 53, 60, 66, 67, 72–77, 127, 131, 150, 155, 158, 216, 217, 225, 226, 234, 235 etc., 238, 240, 244, 250, 263
Furness, W. H., 102, 166

G

Gannett, E. S., 65, 160, 166, 213, quoted, 216
Gannett, W. C., 216
Garrison, W. L., 126
Gospels, the, 244
Gray, F. T., 65, 225
Gray, Thomas, 160, 223
Gray, William, 122
Greenwood, F. W. P., 51, 66, 72, 160, 167, 211

H

Hale, E. E., 160, 211, **253**
Hall, E. B., 166
Hall, Nathaniel, 189 etc.
Hamilton, Alex., statue of, 233
Harris, T. M., 160, 190
Harvard College, 18, 19, 159, 201
Hedge, F. H., 72, 102, 129, 160, 234, quoted
Hemans, Felicia, 138
Hillard, G. S., 160
Huntington, F. D., 160, 162, quoted

K

Kempis, Thomas à, "De Imitatione Christi," 256
King, T. S., 160
King's Chapel, 227
Kirkland, J. T., 21, 23, 160, 167
Kneeland, Abner, 101

L

Lafayette, 139
Latin School, 20
Law, William, "Serious Call," 256
Lawrence, Abbot, 94
Lawrence, Amos A., 196
Layman, 51
Lecture, Thursday, 31
Libraries in Boston, 19
Lincoln, Abraham, 198
Literary Spirit, 90
London, 140
Longfellow, H. W., 145, 159, 198
Lothrop, S. K., 68, 160
Lotteries, 113–115
Lowell, Charles, 66, 160
Lowell, J. R., 170
Lunt, W. P., 11, 51, 72, 160, 171, 265

M

Macaulay, T. B., 141
Martineau, James, 56
Mather, Increase, 69
May, S. J., 49
McKean, Joseph, 22, 27
Men, Distinguished, among the Unitarians, 259
Meyerbeer, 142
Milman, H. H., 144
Milton, John, 200
Morton, Charles, 219
Myers, F. W, H., quoted, 91

N

Napoleon III., 153
Norton, Andrews, 55, 70, 139, 207, 211, 244, 245

O

Old and New, the, 208, 211
Old World and New, 130, 156
Orleans, Maid of, 143, 149

P

Paine, Thomas, 226
Palfrey, J. G., 2, 23, 72, 76, 160, 181, 190, 240
Paris, 142, 143
Parker, Theodore, 1, 8, 13, 33, 34, 39, 55, 57, 59, 62, 64, 69, 70, 101, 155, 160, 168, 179, 187, 193, 204, 209, 218, 249–251, 256, 264
Parkman, Francis, 21, 66, 129, 160, 161 etc., 190, 224
Peabody, A. P., 71, 181, 190
Peabody, Elizabeth, 6, 7
Peabody, Ephraim, 160
Peabody, W. B. O., 72
Peace, Congress, 149–152
Perkins, James, 19, 94

Phillips, W., 126, 197
Pierce, John, 22, 160, 219, 224
Pierpont, John, 64, 160, 184 etc., 193
Porter, Eliphalet, 160
Prescott, W. H., 94, 159, 201
Priestley, Joseph, 18, 248
Putnam, A. P., 175, 261
Putnam, George, 160, 190

R

Rachel, 142, 153
Register, Christian, 212
Renan, Ernest, 3, 242
Repository and Review, 207
Rheims, 149
Rhine, the, 145
Ripley, George, 13, 160, 193, 251, 264, 265
Robbins, Chandler, 72, 160, 177 etc., 218
Rogers, Samuel, 141
Romanism, 133

S

Saint Cloud, 151
Sewall, Samuel, 93
Shaw, Lemuel, 94, 101
Slavery, 194, 198
Society (Port), 66
Society (Seaman's Aid), 66
Sparks, Jared, 23, 160
Story Joseph, 101
Sumner, Charles, 126, 199

T

Tappan, Lewis, 65
Terracina, 132
Thacher, Judge S. C., 167
Theological Decomposition, 226
Thompson, J. W., 190

Ticknor, George, 19, 159, 201
Transcendentalism, 264, 265
Treves, 148
Tuckerman, Joseph, 65

U

Union, the, 198
Union (Young Men's Christian), 66
Unitarian Charities, 127
Unitarian Controversy, 67
Unitarianism, 1, 23, 38, 69, 193, 200, 204, 227, 240 etc., 265
Unitarianism, the New, 259, 266, 267
Unitarian Liberality, 127
Unitarian Moral Sentiment, 156, 157
Unitarian Piety, 256
Universalism, 227

V

Verses by N. L. Frothingham, 78–85, 88, 89, 128, 130, 157, 172–174, 181, 197, 247

W

Wales, T. B., 94
Walker, James, 2, 50, 65, 71, 72, 102, 160, 183, 211, 240, 265
Ware, H., Jr., 65, 102, 160, 164, 180, 256
Wasson, D. A., 193
Webber, Samuel, 20
Webster, Daniel, 94, 126, 196, 197, 201
Webster, Noah, 19
Weiss, John, 193
Westminster Abbey, 136
Whipple, E. P., 164
White, D. A., 101
Willson, E. B., 193
Winthrop, John, 200, 201
Winthrop, R. C., 167, 170
Worship, Places of, in Boston (1811), 48

Y

Young, Alexander, 2, 66, 72, 160, 166 etc., 225, 240

www.ingramcontent.com/pod-product-compliance
Lightning Source LLC
Chambersburg PA
CBHW051647040426
42446CB00009B/1010